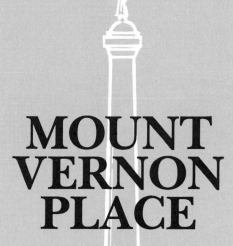

MOUNT VERNON PLACE

An Anecdotal Essay with 66 Illustrations

John Dorsey

MACLAY & ASSOCIATES INC.

Baltimore • 1983

Acknowledgments

It was Harold A. Williams, my editor for 19 years at the Sunday Sun, *who assigned me the task of preparing an article on the history of Mount Vernon Place for the* Sun Magazine. *That article appeared in two parts on June 7 and 14, 1970. Mr. Williams, before his retirement from the* Sun, *also secured for me the* Sunpapers' *gracious permission to use that article as the basis for this version.*

I wish I could remember all those who so kindly helped me on the original article; but as that was a long time ago I must ask them to forgive me if I try only to mention those who have been in some way involved with this book. Among them are:

The Enoch Pratt Free Library, for granting permission to use material from the booklet, "Mr. Peabody's Library", which I wrote in 1978 and to which the library holds the copyright; and to Averil Kadis, of the library's public relations department, for securing the permission. As the wording is not the same here, I have not used quotation marks around the Peabody material, but it is largely taken from the 1978 booklet.

The Peabody Library and its director, Lyn Hart, for permission to use the picture of the interior of the library which originally appeared in the provost's report of 1879.

The Walters Art Gallery and its public relations director, Jonathan Rogers, for generously supplying information, and for supplying as well slides from which a number of the pictures in this book were made.

Ann Deckret and Lynn Cox (director) of the print and photograph department of the Peale Museum, for much help in locating pictures from the Peale collection and having them reproduced.

Laurie Baty and Paula Velthuys (director) of the Maryland Historical Society's prints and photographs department, for much help in finding pictures from that collection and having them reproduced.

Ann Garside, the Peabody Institute's public relations director, for information about the Peabody's plans for 27-33 East Mount Vernon Place.

For generously sharing with me their knowledge, so many people, including Douglas H. Gordon, Jr.; Francis Jencks; Mrs. John Baylor; professor Garrett Power of the University of Maryland Law School (author of the forthcoming "High Society", a study of the 70-foot zoning law, which will appear in a future issue of the Maryland Historical Magazine); *Mrs. Shirley Wiesand of 15 West Mount Vernon Place; Jere Santry, manager of the Engineering Society of Baltimore; The Rev. Kenneth S. Jones, pastor of the Mount Vernon Place Methodist Church; Dr. Hugh F. Hicks, owner of four properties on Mount Vernon and Washington Places; T. W. Swank, resident manager of the Washington Apartments; Dr. Nicholas Iliff, of 14 West Mount Vernon Place; William R. Johnston, of the Walters Art Gallery.*

Robert W. Armacost, for reading the manuscript and making valuable suggestions, and for even more valuable encouragement along the way.

And to Richard and Lyn Hart, whose intelligence and insight have given this effort whatever readability it may have, a gratitude which, great as it is and has been on similar occasions, always seems to me inadequate.

Finally, I think some acknowledgment is due my publisher, John Maclay, whose duties are certainly many and varied. It was he who first suggested the possibility of this project, and from that time about a year and a half ago to this he has acted as astute editor of the work and designer of the book as well as assuming all of the financial and other obligations that go with being a publisher. Above all as far as I am concerned, he has brought a great enthusiasm to the effort, which has made it all as much fun as possible.

The responsibility for any errors which may have survived the contributions of all these people is, of course, entirely mine.

J. D.

Foreword

First off, I must try to explain what this is and what it isn't. By Mount Vernon Place is meant the four squares around the Washington Monument. Actually, the first blocks of East and West Monument Street, from St. Paul Street on the east to Cathedral Street on the west, comprise Mount Vernon Place; and the 600 and 700 blocks North Charles Street, from Centre Street on the south to Madison Street on the north, comprise Washington Place. In practice, however, all four squares are usually referred to as Mount Vernon Place. "Mount Vernon" has lent its name to the surrounding area as well, but except for an occasional reference to something across the street, I propose to deal here only with the four parks, their enclosing buildings, and some of the people whose lives have contributed to the history of this small but significant piece of Baltimore. That alone is far too large a task for a project of this size.

And that brings me to the second important point to be made at the outset. This essay makes no attempt to be a complete history. I hope it will be taken for what it says it is, an anecdotal essay.

for Bob

There," wrote Henry James in 1904, "were the best houses, the older, the ampler, the more blandly quadrilateral; which in spite of their still faces met one's arrest, at their commodious corners and other places of vantage, with an unmistakable *manner*....A certain vividness of high decency seemed....to possess them, and this suggestion of the real Southern glow, yet with no Southern looseness, was clearly something by itself...."

The "there" referred to by James in his great essay on Baltimore was Mount Vernon Place, or more correctly Mount Vernon and Washington Places, the four squares with their enclosing buildings which provide a cruciform setting for the Washington Monument. They are handsome, these squares; taken together, they comprise what has been called one of the finest urban spaces in America. But Mount Vernon Place, the name generally used to denote all four squares, is more than that. Baltimoreans have long thought of it as the heart of their city, its Piazza San Marco, for reasons deeper than the physical. If one were to attempt to know a city one would perhaps begin by walking its streets and looking at its buildings, and go on from there to a study of its history. But the real search would be for things less palpable, more fundamental: its character, its spirit, itself. In Mount Vernon Place are to be found all of those things.

It is not a matter of age. There are older parts of Baltimore. But it is a matter of time, or one might better say of timing. The history of the growth and prominence of Mount Vernon Place belongs to the Nineteenth Century, and the Nineteenth Century also stands at the center of Baltimore's history. The city traces its beginnings to 1729, but it was not until after the Revolution that Baltimore was anything more than a little port overshadowed by Annapolis. Between 1800 and 1900 Baltimore became one of the major cities of the United States. That was when most of the great fortunes were made here, most of the great philanthropies bestowed. That was when the city formed its architectural character and its historical essence, which, despite the changes of our own century, remain much as they were. Baltimore, that is to say, became an adult in the Nineteenth Century, and, like you or me, no matter how long it may live after that development, its character is not likely to change much.

One of the reasons Mount Vernon Place is so representative of that character is that, while many other parts of the city have been visited by the builders and rebuilders since 1900, these squares have changed hardly at all in terms of their buildings. Thus one can see here a fascinating record of many of the Nineteenth Century's architectural styles. In the early decades Baltimore was a leader of the neoclassical style popularly known as Greek Revival, and one of that style's best architects, Robert Mills, made his name here with the Washington Monument before going on to bigger commissions in the nation's capital, including the great obelisk on the Mall. From Mills's column and the Greek Revival townhouse, the architectural record of Mount Vernon Place proceeds through echoes of the Italian Renaissance, a passion for brownstone facades, the Gothic Revival, and on down to Stanford White's fashionable eclecticism, the Beaux Arts, the Chateauesque, and even a touch of John Russell Pope, whose Roman pomp was popular at the turn of the century and for decades afterwards. If Mills, White and Pope are in national terms the most important architects associated with Mount Vernon Place, others whose names are known locally and beyond include Niernsee and Neilson, Josias Pennington, Edmund G. Lind, Dixon and Carson, Charles E. Cassell, Joseph Evans Sperry, E. H. Glidden, Delano and Aldrich, Carrere and Hastings.

But what was built here is only the beginning of what Mount Vernon Place has to reveal. It is the history, the accumulated life, that gives the Place its depth of sensation. G. K. Chesterton, after he visited here, wrote of "the thronging of thousands of living thoughts and things" which made their presence felt on Mount Vernon Place. Henry James called it the city's "parlour," and compared the Washington Monument to an overlarge antique clock that sits in the "parlour" generation after generation, silently witnessing the family history. As the "parlour" is the most important room in the house, so from the mid-Nineteenth Century until the First World War Mount Vernon Place was the most important, the most desirable, and probably the most expensive place in town to live. It was the home of many of the most eminent members of the upper class when that class ran things, here as elsewhere. And so it was where a disproportionate number of significant events took place, a disproportionate number of important visitors visited, a disproportionate number of those perhaps minor but delightful stories which give a city's history its liveliness had their origin. Gertrude Stein said of Oakland, California, "There is no there there." One can say of Mount Vernon Place that there is more *there* there than there is anywhere else in town.

There the Walterses collected and Peabody built and Francis Scott Key died and Thackeray ate terrapin and Henry Pratt Janes sued over a vestibule and the men of the 29th Division marched when they came home from the war to end war.

There the Prince of Wales, later Edward VII, was entertained; and the Duke of Windsor, formerly Edward VIII, stayed when he visited Baltimore with his wife, formerly Wallis Warfield, who played there as a child. There a boarding house was host to Jerome Bonaparte, grandson of that other Jerome Bonaparte (brother of Napoleon) who married that other Baltimorean, Betsy Patterson. The same boarding house was also host to Woodrow Wilson in the 1880's when he was studying at Johns Hopkins (just up the street in those days); thirty years later, when he was President, Wilson again stayed on Mount Vernon Place, this time in the house of Theodore Marburg, where, it is said, the two men drafted the covenant of the League of Nations. Other Presidents came to Mount Vernon Place, too, as we shall see.

There Harry Lehr and Louise Morris went wading through a fountain on their way home from a ball in the Nineties, and everybody was *terribly amused*; but when in the

1940's another man, who later gave his name as Smith, took off all his clothes and went dancing in the fountain, no one was amused and he spent the night in jail despite his protest that "there are statues up there with no clothes on."

There a member of Congress was journalistically transported one night early in this century, because it was so respectable. He had got into a fight in a house of ill repute in a less distinguished neighborhood, and was bashed over the head with a spitoon. The injury necessitated a trip to the hospital, so it couldn't be kept out of the newspapers; but H. L. Mencken and the other young journalists of the day, more discreet than present-day reporters, agreed to save the poor man embarrassment and ascribed the accident to a fall on the ice on Mount Vernon Place. But some 30 years later the Place had its own house of ill repute for a time, when it was at its lowest ebb.

Mount Vernon Place has had its ups and downs. Had it not, it would reflect its city less well. But the fact that it remains, intact, is more than a testament to the latter-day preservationists, though it is certainly that. The commemorative statues, which led one resident to call the Place "our municipal Pantheon," have been accumulating there for a hundred years or more; they show that even a century ago Mount Vernon Place was thought of as more than a nice address—then as now it had a special significance to Baltimore.

The sense of the special comes in part from the beauty of design, in part from the presence of major institutions, in part from the sense of history; but this Place reflects Baltimore, is indeed its symbolic embodiment, because of other things, too, things that have to do with living, and with scale, and with attitude.

Back in the Twenties Mencken wrote a piece in which he deplored the building of skyscrapers in Baltimore. Baltimore, his argument went, shouldn't try to be like New York because it couldn't be. It should be satisfied with being Baltimore, which he thought was better anyway. New York was a place where people transacted business; if they had to reside there, they did so meanly, in big impersonal apartment houses. Baltimore, on the other hand, was a place where people lived — in houses, which were of human scale and which made the people in them feel comfortable, at home.

Mount Vernon Place says just that. It is to a great degree a place of houses, where people lived; people still do live in many of them. New York is often symbolized by Wall Street, where people do business. Washington is usually symbolized by the Capitol, where people govern. Baltimore is symbolized by Mount Vernon Place, where people live.

Moreover, because the scale of Mount Vernon Place is that of the house — with but a couple of exceptions the buildings are no taller than the townhouse of a well-to-do person — it is a scale in which the human being can feel comfortable and at home rather than overwhelmed and insignificant.

And that is the kind of place Baltimore is. Those of us who love the city will tell you that we love it precisely because it is not New York or London or Paris. It is smaller, quieter, more comfortable and homey, more conservative in its ways; the mind is better able to compass it and feel, in some nonphysical sense, secure here. There is nothing particularly exciting about Mount Vernon Place, but Baltimoreans don't especially like excitement, and the tension that goes with it. They like to be comfortable. And they like to be at home. Literally. Baltimoreans are stay-at-homes to an astonishing degree for inhabitants of a city this large. And when they do go out the place they like best to go is to somebody else's home, for dinner. As the "parlour," in James's singularly apt image, is the center of the home, so Mount Vernon Place in its scale and in its meaning is the spiritual center of this very homey city.

But that isn't all. Mount Vernon Place also reflects the Baltimorean's self-serving reserve, what I have elsewhere called his smug inhibition. We are often accused, when we talk of liking our city because it isn't bigger and more exciting, of a provincial defensiveness. And to a degree that may be true. Now and then we may be secretly inclined to wish that Baltimore were, well, at least a little more important, more noticed among the cities of the world. But we would never admit that to a New Yorker. There is in us, as there is in everybody, that which wants to be noticed; but there is in us also, and more strongly, that which doesn't want to *seem* to want to be noticed. So our public attitude must be that we like our city just as it is; were it more it would be — not quite proper. Mount Vernon Place says — above all and precisely — that.

The scale of these little squares, both of the parks and of the buildings facing them, is such that it projects, and as a virtue, that it is not *more*. The houses are large, for they were the houses of the rich, but they never matched in size or grandeur the palaces of upper Fifth Avenue or Newport — and not only because Baltimoreans were not, by and large, as rich as Vanderbilts or Rockefellers. No, these facades have about them a certain reserve, a certain disinclination to demand attention. Taken together, they suggest the traditional Baltimore attitude: partly English, partly Southern, partly that of the wallflower who has convinced herself that it's better not to have a crowd of men around. From a history of being overlooked, Baltimoreans have decided that being overlooked was what they had in mind all the time. "Admire me if you will," say the houses on Mount Vernon Place, "but don't get the idea that I care." Even the biggest house there, designed by Stanford White and John Russell Pope for the most pretentious of Baltimore's socialites, exhibits that quality of, in James's phrase, the "blandly quadrilateral." And, as he also implied, the blandly complacent.

Not, however, for the lack of expenditure. I am speaking, of course, of *the* house on Mount Vernon Place, which is just what *the* house most anywhere is: not the oldest or the most beautiful, but the biggest and the most expensive. Its facade stretches 117 feet along the square and takes in three addresses: numbers 7, 9, and 11 West. It is even deeper than it is long, and has been the object of a great many superlatives including "the longest rowhouse in the world" — which, conveniently, it would be difficult to check.

The house, with everything in it, is said to have cost up to $6 million. When you consider that in today's terms that might be 20 times as much, it seems impossible to believe that such a sum could have been spent on it. But the more you know about the house, its mistress, and all that went into it, the less impossible it seems.

Let us take ourselves back to the year when James visited and gathered the impressions for his essay, 1904; the Place was at its apogee, and the final part of the great mansion at 7, 9, and 11 had just been completed. Let us pretend that we have been invited by the mistress of the house to take a tour — quite an honor, as we shall see. The house, as we have been told in preparation for our visit, was originally three separate rowhouses, built at mid-century. In 1872 the lady who is our hostess married one of Baltimore's richer men, whose father bought the newlyweds number 11 as a wedding present. In time, though they had no children, the house became too small for their style of living; so they bought the house next door, number 9, and hired one of America's leading architects, Stanford White of New York, to turn both into a single residence. Some years later our hostess's first husband died, and in 1902 she married the man who had been his doctor. At that point, though there were still no children, the house again seemed too small, and the lady whom we are visiting, since she's the rich one, bought the next house down, number 7, and hired the presently popular young architect John Russell Pope to make it an addition to her already ample mansion.

We note as we approach that Pope has extended the brownstone facade across the front of the third house in a manner entirely in keeping with White's design. The entrance is in the westernmost portion, one of the two thirds designed by White. We pass through curved doors of oak and poplar into a vestibule with a mosaic floor, a fountain, and a huge Tiffany window on the front. From there we go into the hall, two stories high, with more Tiffany windows on the upper floor, with oak paneling and an immense fireplace, and with a second-floor gallery running around three sides of the room.

From this room a tight, spiral oak staircase ascends to another Tiffany window two floors above, and beside the staircase there is a rather narrow hall that leads to the family dining room, gloomily impressive with its tapestried walls and elaborately carved, black-painted fireplace and sideboard. Across one corner is one of the house's big vaults, this one no doubt for the family silver. There is plenty of it.

Off the dining room is the ladies' withdrawing room, much lighter in feeling, its domed ceiling delicately decorated with plasterwork and its walls covered in our hostess's favorite color: red.

Going back to the front hall, we pass from there to the second section of the house, originally number 9, also part of the Stanford White design. Here there were two rooms, but they have recently been made into one great drawing room. It is lighter and more airy in feeling this way, though heavy curtains still hang at doors as well as windows and the room is filled with French furniture ordered by Mr. White from Jules Allard Freres in Paris.

From this room two doors lead to the Pope section of the house. One of them goes to the library in front, with its paneling and built-in bookcases, the other to a hall, from which a wide, open marble stairway descends to the ground floor. Looking at this stairway, and comparing it in our minds with White's twisting, wooden design in the other hall, we realize that while Pope may have made his part of the facade conform to White's, he has here expressed his own, very different vision.

To the rear of the hall is a great ballroom, 30 feet wide by 70 feet long, with a large stage at the far end, and a partially gilded ceiling inset with glass panels lighted from above. The upper walls of the room are painted with scenes, and below them are red damask panels on which hang a part of the collection of Old Master paintings which will, when it is complete, include works by Hals, Rembrandt, Van Dyke, Fragonard, Sully, Canaletto, Chardin and others.

Returning to the hall and descending that marble stairway, we come, under the ballroom, to the elegant supper room, where 120 can be seated and where mirrored walls reflect beautiful Meissen chandeliers and sconces.

Overwhelming as this short tour of one floor and one room below has been, we have not seen the house in its final form. In 1913, it will acquire a grand gallery across the back of the main floor which will enclose the square around the house's central, roofed, three-story conservatory, with its cascades of greenery down the walls and its claustrophobia of orchids and other exotic flowers, the whole relieved by a splashing fountain and canaries.

Nor have we met our hostess, the person more responsible than any other for the mansion we have seen and a figure who is in the process of becoming almost legendary among the upper reaches of Baltimore Society. She is, by 1904, Mrs. Henry Barton Jacobs, queen of Society; but she began, 53 years ago, as Mary Sloan Frick.

It was no mean beginning. Miss Frick was the daughter of a well-known lawyer in Baltimore, and came of an old family with connections to the New York Fricks. When she married Robert Garrett in 1872 and moved into number 11 West, Garrett was already a well-known name on the squares. Robert's grandfather, the founder of a famous Baltimore banking house, had earlier lived at 14 or 16 East; and had built for Robert's father, John W., president of the Baltimore and Ohio Railroad, a mansion at the southwest corner of Cathedral and Monument Streets, where the Mount Vernon Place Apartments stand today. The house later belonged to Robert's sister, Miss Mary Garrett, who founded Bryn Mawr School, and eventually the house became the first home of the Baltimore Museum of Art.

When Mary Frick married Robert Garrett she was a good catch. For all their money, the Garretts had not been in Baltimore Society long, and they needed to make alliances with old families.* With Mary Frick, Robert Garrett got a class name, and with the present of the house at 11 West he got a class address to go with it. The house, built about the middle of the Nineteenth Century, had belonged to Samuel K. George, from whom the Garretts bought it. They lived there for a decade before buying 9 West, which had belonged to Captain James Ryan. Captain Ryan was married to Susan Fitzhugh Gordon, which establishes one of the Gordon family connections with the four squares.

See note next page.

The Garretts promptly hired Stanford White to turn the two houses into a single mansion, and turn it he did, to the alarm of the neighbors. If we, today, can see in the Garrett-Jacobs mansion an example of Baltimore reserve, to the owners of its staid, mid-century neighbors it was too, too modern.

Especially opposed to it was the Garretts' next-door neighbor, Henry Pratt Janes, who lived at 13 West. When it became evident that the Garretts' vestibule would protrude from the former building line and cut off Mr. Janes's view of the Washington Monument from his first floor windows, he sued — on the basis of deprivation of view and deprivation of "air and sunlight." Lest those reasons sound silly, rowhouses do need as much sunlight as possible through their front windows, as they don't have side windows in the front rooms; and after all, one of the reasons people wanted to live on Mount Vernon Place was for the view of the nationally-famous Washington Monument.

A lower court took Mr. Janes's suit seriously, and decided in his favor. But the Garretts appealed and finally prevailed in a higher court after the testimony of John R. Niernsee that there was nothing wrong with the house or its vestibule. Thirty years later Mrs. Garrett, who was by then Mrs. Jacobs, was to buy 13 West and tear down all but the front part of it for the final addition to her house, a pantry. Oh, yes, and to provide the west side of her house with additional "light and air." The mills of the rich sometimes grind slowly, but they grind exceeding well.

If Stanford White is the architect of record of the first two parts of the house, it is said that there were many disputes with the imperious Mary Garrett, and some think she is equally responsible for its appearance. In any case, as we have seen, when she bought number 7 West in 1902 she hired not Stanford White, who was still alive, but John Russell Pope as architect.

By that time, she was Mrs. Jacobs. Robert Garrett did not enjoy good health. In the

*The Garretts had, of course, bought their way into Society just the way everybody else has for thousands of years. Many of today's oldest and most distinguished families are descended from people who, in medieval times, bought their way in by scraping together enough money to buy a horse, the prerequisite for becoming a knight and starting up the ladder. Buying your way in got a bad name in America because the only real class system in this country is economic; at some point, therefore, those who had been rich but no longer were had to create some fiction other than money to keep themselves in. They therefore created the fiction of blood. The fiction was reinforced in the South, to which Baltimore has strong ties, after the Civil War, when there were an awful lot of people down there who had been rich but no longer were. The term "genteel poverty" became quite popular. But of course the strongest advocates of the fiction of blood have always been the sons and daughters of those who bought their way in. The standard procedure is to make enough money to buy your way in so that your children can try and keep their generation's nouveaux riches out with the fiction that Society is based on blood, not money. They don't succeed, and so the wheel rolls on.

late 1880's his health broke down completely. At that point Dr. Henry Barton Jacobs, a Boston specialist, was brought in to be his personal physician. To be near his patient, Dr. Jacobs moved to Baltimore and maintained an office in the Garrett house, entered through the still-existing door to the ground floor at the west end of it. Dr. Jacobs no doubt prolonged Mr. Garrett's life, but could not do so indefinitely. Robert Garrett died in 1896. Six years later — after a suitable interval even for those days — the widow married Dr. Jacobs, who gave up the active practice of medicine and settled down to being a civic-minded citizen.

Even better bred than his wife — he was directly descended from John and Priscilla Alden and related to five other Mayflower passengers — Dr. Jacobs was a quiet, intelligent, conservative, beautifully-educated man. He was a founder of the Maryland Tuberculosis Association, a contributor to numerous medical societies, a longterm vestryman of Grace and St. Peter's Church, vice president and president of the board of the Baltimore Museum, a member of every important club in the city and of at least 20 boards of directors, a well-known figure in European as well as American medical circles, and the collector of 5,000 books on medical subjects, which filled the shelves in the big library.

But withal he did not compete — indeed, he did not try to — with his wife. Their marriage on April 2, 1902 came as something of a shock to the community, despite many rumors. A week before, the then Mrs. Garrett (51) had been asked by a newspaper if her engagement to Dr. Jacobs (43) was about to be announced. "There will be no such announcement," she replied succinctly, and that seemed to settle the matter. True to her word, there was no such announcement. One day they just went over to Grace and St. Peter's and got married. Even the household servants were taken by surprise.

The previous day, the couple had signed a legal agreement that neither would ever claim any of the other's possessions. That must have been to satisfy the lady, for she had many times the money he had. She was reputed to be worth $20,000,000 in 1902, and some have put her fortune, at its greatest, at a much higher figure.

It has been said that she made most of it herself. The story goes that at the time of the near-collapse of the B. & O., in the 1880's, she offered to buy all of Miss Mary Garrett's stock in the railroad, and did, when it was selling very low. It was a gamble, for the line went into a form of receivership, and Mrs. Garrett is said to have spent many hours pacing the floor in anxiety over whether she had done the right thing. She had. The B. & O.'s finances were put in order, the railroad subsequently prospered, and Mrs. Garrett made a fortune. Or so the story goes.

She spent her money, or a lot of it, consolidating her position at the acme of Baltimore Society — efforts which only continued after she married Dr. Jacobs. It was *Mrs.* Henry Barton Jacobs, the papers reported, who bought the house at 7 West and rebuilt it as an addition to *her* mansion. It was Mrs. Jacobs who owned a villa at Newport (also designed by John Russell Pope), who owned an estate called Uplands near Catonsville, who kept an apartment in Paris, who collected the notable paintings

— or at least paid for them — which decorated those gold and red walls of hers.

(About the art collection, it has been reported that in 1908 René Gimpel, a Paris art dealer, informed Mrs. Jacobs that a number of her French paintings were fakes. Presumably she got rid of them, and subsequently, it is reported, she bought through M. Gimpel.)

She not only collected art. She collected more than 100 Oriental rugs for her floors, loads and loads of furniture (most of it, curiously, seems to have been reproduction, not authentic Eighteenth Century French furniture), and enough other stuff to outfit a moderate-sized town. A catalogue of the auction sale of the effects of the house, held in 1940 after both Jacobses had died, is revealing.

The auction, which went on for days, contained 1,210 lots. Among them were 107 lots of china (many of them whole services) including 232 entree plates, 485 dinner plates, and 664 dessert plates; 1,147 wine glasses and finger bowls; 124 lots of linens; 78 lots of silver plus 49 lots of Georgian silver and Sheffield plate; 58 lots of decorative porcelain and faience; 46 lots of bronzes, ormolu and terra cottas; 155 gilded music room chairs (the ballroom was also used for recitals and musicales); 86 table cloths of various sizes, not counting a 7-yard banquet cloth and a 9-yard banquet cloth, and on and on. And Mrs. Jacobs had two other houses and an apartment in Paris.

She also had a staff of servants, for the Mount Vernon Place mansion, which numbered between 16 and 24. The lower, plainer level of the now-disused two-level elevator was for the menials; the upper level, plushly upholstered, was for family and guests. This was one of the curiosities of the house, another of which was the interesting early form of air conditioning. Above the ballroom stage there remains a huge fan, which the present owners of the building made the mistake of turning on when they moved in. It pulled clouds of accumulated soot out of the hot-air heating ducts, and the cleanup job took days.

Mrs. Jacobs seems to have been a restless person, always changing the decorations of her various residences. As soon as something was finished, she wanted to change it. And like the others of her time who had the money to do so, she was always moving from place to place. The summer was spent in Newport, the fall at Uplands, the winter "season" at Mount Vernon Place, the spring in Europe. But getting to Europe, for Mrs. Jacobs, was less than half the fun: she got seasick. And so to make the ordeal as bearable as possible she had her staterooms, in whatever ship she decided to take, redecorated with her own furniture and hangings. On board with her went also a special supply of the foods she liked best, which were prepared in a special galley by special stewards.

When she traveled by carriage, and later by car, she was accompanied by two servants, a chauffeur and a footman. Once, going to Bar Harbor on vacation, she took along 8 horses, 2 Victorias, a dog cart, a vis-a-vis, 4 wagons, and 100 trunks and boxes. When she went to the Chicago World's Fair in 1893 the arrangements for the accommodations for her party of 8 required 40 letters and 16 telegrams. She reserved 2 single bedrooms, 3 double bedrooms, 3 servants' rooms, 3 bathrooms, and, oddly enough, only 1 sitting room. Her rooms, she specified, "are to have fireplaces and to face the lake."

Mary Frick Garrett Jacobs had her rivals in Baltimore Society from time to time. "Almighty Lou" Gill was the principal one for a time (and wouldn't it be nice to know more about someone with a nickname like that?), and there was a fun-loving crowd gathered around the "Allie" (Alexander) Browns who didn't go in for the stuffiness of the Jacobs set. (Indeed, Douglas Gordon recalls that "Mrs. Alexander Brown once said, 'I could sleep with a different man every night and people would still come to my parties.' And she was right, because she was a fascinating woman.")

But stuffy or not, Mrs. Jacobs spent money on a scale that was simply beyond serious competition in Baltimore. And so, of course, she was the queen of Society, the grandest ever of our grande dames (for as the late William B. Marye once succinctly put it, "Baltimore loves money"). If she so much as acknowledged you, with a little bow in your direction at the opera or the races, you felt your social position rise a little. If she dropped in on your party for a few minutes it was a success. And if she invited you to her house you had it made. After she and a group of other ladies founded the Assembly — still one of the most exclusive functions of the social season (some would say *the* most exclusive) — it was said that the committee designated to decide on who got invitations never really had the final say: Mrs. Jacobs did.

Mrs. John Nicholas Brown, who grew up in Baltimore as Anne Kinsolving, recalls a story about the Assembly and Mrs. Jacobs. "I remember somebody wrote a play about a meeting of the Assembly committee. In the play the meeting took place in the 'throne room' of the Henry Barton Jacobs house, and Queen Mary Jacobs was sitting on the throne and Mathilde Manly, the first lady-in-waiting, entered singing, 'Hail, Mary, full of checks.'"

There is a story, perhaps apochryphal but from more than one source, that one day a lady was ushered into The Presence of Mrs. Jacobs and seated herself in a large armchair. The visitor thought she felt something wriggling under her, but was far too self-conscious in The Presence to jump up; so she reasoned that she was imagining things. After a few minutes the wriggling stopped and the lady relaxed, thinking her aberration had passed. When she rose to leave it was discovered that she had smothered one of Mrs. Jacobs's pet Pekingese dogs. (I wish I knew what she did then.)

Another lady, who made her debut in the Teens and was entertained by Mrs. Jacobs, has recalled her tellingly as "a formal and a formidable woman." But if her formality and all that went with it seems a bit ridiculous to the present generation, it wasn't to our grandfathers and great-grandfathers. It was what people, at least people in Society, did. No one thought Mrs. Jacobs absurd; she was a representative product of her time, a time when rich people thought nothing of sitting down several times a week to sumptuous meals of seven courses, including oysters, terrapin at $12 a portion, and canvasback ducks. If Mrs. Jacobs had more servants than anybody else in Baltimore, those who lived on Mount Vernon Place couldn't possibly get by without at least seven.

This wonderfully atmospheric shot is from an unknown date about the turn of the century. There is an aura of peacefulness here which, whether accurately or inaccurately, we associate with the late Nineteenth Century.

West Mount Vernon Place about 1886, after the building of the first two-thirds of the Garrett-Jacobs mansion and after the William Walters gift of Barye sculptures. The lion is at center, and the Walters house second from left. In the background is the side of the Mary Garrett house at Cathedral and Monument Streets.

Unlike the familiar, sweet-looking portrait of Mrs. Henry Barton Jacobs, this photograph, taken in London, has not been seen in many years, if in fact it has ever been published before. Unlike the portrait, too, it shows her more in the "Queen Mary" attitude.

This great pile, the Garrett-Jacobs house (now the Engineering Center of Baltimore) was built in two stages, but you can't tell it from this facade. The right two-thirds were created by Stanford White in 1884, the left third was added by John Russell Pope in 1902. Pope's concept can be seen to be different when one is inside, but he deferred to White on the facade. The house once had a balustrade running across the top.

The ballroom of the Garrett-Jacobs mansion about the turn of the century, with the portrait of the Prince Regent, later George IV of England, at the far end of the stage. The Jacobs art collection is now at the Baltimore Museum of Art.

The Garrett house, on the southwest corner of Cathedral and Monument Streets, where the Mount Vernon Apartments now stand, was built in 1862. It is in many ways obviously a copy of One West, especially the portico and double stairway. When this picture was taken in the 1920's, shortly before it was torn down, it was the home of the Baltimore Museum of Art.

But people didn't only spend on themselves. Mrs. Jacobs, for instance, was conscious of her social obligations. She gave $40,000 to this charity, $50,000 to that one. Childless herself, she enjoyed endowing hospitals for children, and every Christmas gave a party at her house for all Baltimore's messenger boys. Before she died she gave her art collection, then appraised at $2,000,000, to the Baltimore Museum of Art. And when she died in 1936 she left Uplands as a home for aged Episcopal women and most of the rest of her $6,000,000 estate (it would have been many times that before the Depression) to charity. Furthermore she did not, by the standards of her time, flaunt her wealth or her position. We have lingered long with her because her style of living was indicative of, if grander than, the way most people on Mount Vernon Place lived in those days. They lived big but they didn't advertise it. They were shy about that, and with reason. The lower classes, you know. The story is told of the newly-rich man in New York who built a mansion with gold-plated doors on the front. When a friend suggested he change to a duller metal so as not to invite the resentment of the lower classes, he did so. He changed to platinum. Mrs. Jacobs's doors were neither gold nor platinum. She never sought publicity; when she could, she shunned it. She never gave interviews to the newspapers. Perish the thought.

If she was shy of the press, however, she was not so shy as her next-door neighbor, Henry Walters. He lived in the smaller but handsome house at number 5 West. When, during the First World War, Henry Walters had his picture taken as a member of the Railway Advisory Board, the *Wall Street Journal* reported that it was the first picture taken of him since he was four years old (the *Wall Street Journal*, for once, was wrong). He was then in his sixties, controlled major railroads in the South, was considered the richest man living below the Mason-Dixon line and owned one of the greatest private art collections in the world. Yet he was so self-effacing that the *Journal* reported, "Walters might be called the Wall Street mystery if enough were known about him to stimulate general curiosity. But. . .he is not even a mystery. He is an unknown."

So great was his passion for anonymity that he would not even answer letters from *Who's Who* and similar publications, though they threatened to print the misinformation they had if he would not correct it. On the other hand, he built his own gallery to house his immense collections and periodically threw it open to the public (always charging a nominal admission, which he always gave to charity), and the range of his buying was far greater than that of more famous collectors such as Mrs. Isabella Stewart Gardner of Boston or Mrs. Potter Palmer of Chicago.

He did not buy indiscriminately, but there were times when he bought voluminously. In 1902, for instance, he bought the Dom Marcello Massarenti collection of early Italian art, up to and including Raphael. It consisted of some 900 works, and Mr. Walters chartered a ship to transport it to America. He usually bought whole collections, in fact — George Lucas, who had been his father's agent, sold him some things, too, but he also bought from Leon Gruel, Dikran Kelekian and other dealers. But his own interests led him to buy some things individually. Richard H. Randall, former director of the Walters, mentions the example of his docking his yacht at St. Petersburg and going to the showrooms of Faberge to select a few items. And the story is told that on his wedding trip he spent days in his hotel room poring over a medieval manuscript he had just purchased. The story is the more believable when you know that on his wedding trip he was 73.

His collection became almost as famous as he was unknown. Whenever there was news of the sale of a European masterpiece to an unknown buyer, the speculation was that Mr. Walters had bought it. Confirmation, though, had to await the next opening of the gallery, for Mr. Walters made no announcements.

It is difficult to imagine that such a collection could be an avocation, but it must be remembered that Mr. Walters directed a huge railroad empire. The beginnings of both empire and collection were made by his father, William T. Walters, who was born in Liverpool, Pennsylvania, in 1820. The son of a banker and merchant, he grew up in Thompsontown, Pennsylvania, where he lived in his mother's family's house, built about 1800 and to this day owned by members of the Thompson family.

He came to Baltimore in 1841 and shortly thereafter founded William T. Walters and Company, the liquor firm from which he made his first significant money. Later he had interests in a Maryland and Pennsylvania Railway called the Northern Central. At the outbreak of the Civil War he took his wife and children to Europe to escape the consequences of his Southern sympathies. He was, in fact, arrested and detained in New York just before he was to sail; but he was a friend of Lincoln's first Secretary of War, Simon Cameron, who secured his release.

After the war he returned to Baltimore and concentrated his major energies on the reconstruction and consolidation of railroads in the South, beginning with the purchase of the Wilmington (North Carolina) and Weldon Railroad and gradually building the system that became the Atlantic Coast Line. After his death in 1894, his son Henry joined forces with J. P. Morgan to buy up more railroad and steamship lines and vastly increased the size and scope of the Atlantic Coast Line. The father and son were active in various other businesses here and elsewhere, including the Safe Deposit Company, which later became the Mercantile Safe Deposit and Trust Company. But it is their art collecting for which they are remembered.

William Walters always claimed that he spent the first $5 he made on a painting. We know which one it was, a painting by E. A. Odier of Napoleon crossing the Alps, but it is no longer in the collection because at some point the gallery sold it. Pity.

During the pre-Civil War period, Mr. Walters was a major collector of contemporary art, interested in such painters as Asher B. Durand and John Kensett. But most of that collection was sold in Europe during the Civil War, probably because Mr. Walters needed the money. Among the works he kept are the more than two hundred watercolors by Alfred Jacob Miller of Miller's trip to the West in 1837, which fortunately the Walters still has.

During his stay in Paris and after his return to Baltimore, Mr. Walters was primarily interested in French Nineteenth Century academic painting by such artists as Gerome and Meissonier — the sort of stuff that's always threatening to make a comeback and maybe finally is doing so — and was the greatest patron of the animalist sculptor Antoine-Louis Barye, of whose works the Walters now owns more than 150 bronzes and many in other media. In 1885 Mr. Walters gave to the city of Baltimore the four groups by Barye — War, Peace, Force, and Order — which reside on the ends of the balustrades to the east and west of the Washington Monument, and the beautiful seated lion in the west square, all of which were unveiled in Mount Vernon Place on February 1 of that year. (It would be nice to have some sort of recognition of their 100th anniversary there.) Mr. Walters also gave the statue of Roger Brooke Taney by William Henry Rinehart that is in the north square, a copy of the original which he gave to Annapolis, and the statue entitled Military Courage, by P. Dubois, which is in the west square. All of these gifts were made in the 1880's.

About this time Mr. Walters was also busily putting together a large collection of Oriental art of which the most famous piece is the Peach Bloom Vase, just 13 inches tall, for which he paid $18,000 in 1886. It was the highest price paid for such a piece to that time, and caused an uproar in New York art circles. It even caused a lawsuit; when one paper called it the most beautiful object ever created by the hand of man, or words to that effect, another paper took exception, and the argument heated up until one paper sued the other. Mr. Walters, who like his son hated publicity, couldn't have been pleased. But he had the vase.

It has been mentioned that William Walters's first purchase was a painting of Napoleon. He seems to have had something of a fixation, for his favorite painting is supposed to have been that of Napoleon in 1814, by Meissonier; and his last purchase, just before he died, was of some portrait miniatures that had belonged to Napoleon. This fixation was complemented by his personality. Imperious, aloof, cold, he was not a favorite of his family. His nieces recalled with displeasure having to wear black silk stockings and white gloves when they were taken to see him at his house on Mount Vernon Place, because that is what he thought little girls ought to wear.

In terms of personality his son was quite different. To those who knew him well, Henry was a genial man. Father and son must have got on, for though William Walters made his son write essays on art as a child these exercises did not turn Henry away from art. William and Henry were both endowed with business acumen and the collector's fervor. But the tastes of the two were quite different.

Even in William Walters's time, the art became far too much for the house at 5 West. In the 1880's he added a gallery to the rear of the building (it now connects the house, used as offices, with the present gallery). The house had been designed shortly before 1850 by the well-known Baltimore architects Niernsee and Neilson. It was owned by the Howard family, leased to John Higgins Duvall for a time, and sold to William Walters in 1871.

Despite the gallery addition, the collection was growing far too large for the property, and when, after William's death in 1894, Henry began to expand the collection vastly in all directions, it became obvious that a lot more space was needed. So Henry bought up the four houses on the west side of South Washington Place, from the alley in back of One West Mount Vernon Place down to Centre Street, with the idea of tearing them down and building a gallery worthy of his art.

Those four houses are gone, but a word about their history is not inappropriate. The earliest, that on the corner, was built by Richard Norris about 1845. His son George Somerville Norris lived there until the Civil War, when he sold the house to Orville Horwitz, a lawyer. The Horwitzes were one of the Jewish families of that time who moved in the highest circles of Baltimore Society. Another were the Benjamin Cohens, who lived near Mount Vernon Place and are reported to have been the first, in 1837, to give a costume ball in Baltimore. Indeed, it seems that Jewish Society and gentile Society mingled to a considerable extent until late in the Nineteenth Century when, for reasons which are not within the scope of this essay, they moved apart.

Number 602 was a fashionable boarding house which opened about 1853 and was run by Miss Eliza Toy. Number 604 was owned by Stephen S. Lee, later by the McCoys of the Maryland White Lead Company, and still later was half of a boarding house run by a Mrs. Turnbull. The other half was number 606, built in 1846 by the son of architect Benjamin Latrobe; it may have been designed by Niernsee. It was at Mrs. Turnbull's that the younger Jerome Bonaparte, and later Woodrow Wilson, lived for a time.

(The second half of the Nineteenth Century seems to have been the age of the boarding house, at least in Baltimore. After the Civil War a number of them were run by ladies who had lost husbands, or fortunes, or both. It was also the age of the "finishing school" for young ladies, and Mount Vernon Place was home to several.)

By 1903 Mr. Walters owned all four of the houses, and was preparing to have them torn down to make way for his gallery when the Great Baltimore Fire intervened in February, 1904. Though the fire didn't come near Mount Vernon Place, it left so many businesses without office space that Mr. Walters agreed to rent the houses as offices for a year. They were demolished in 1905, and the gallery was completed four years later.

The gallery building by Delano and Aldrich has an interior based on the Sixteenth Century Palazzo del Universita (or Palazzo Bianco) in Genoa. It has a distinctly Renaissance look both outside and inside. The central courtyard is a fine architectural achievement. The architect was the young William Delano, a distant relative of Warren Delano, who married Henry Walters's sister, Jennie. The Walters gallery was his first commission.

After the gallery was built, Mr. Walters had more than two decades to live, and he did not stop collecting; that is probably one reason why the building turned out to be large enough to show only 20 per cent of the collection, and why a wing with twice the gallery space became necessary. Although it would seem obvious from this vantage point what Mr. Walters was going to do with his collection, especially after he built the gallery, he never announced his intentions and so it was something of a surprise, after he died in 1931, when it became known that he had left his gallery and his huge collection to the people of Baltimore, together with an endowment to operate it.

Richard Randall asserts that anyone who pays attention to the scope of the collections will have no doubt that Mr. Walters was buying not merely to satisfy his own collecting interests: He all along, according to Mr. Randall, had as his aim the establishment of a great museum.

"Take the armor collection," Mr. Randall has said. "Mr. Walters showed no interest in armor until the Teens, when he was in his sixties. Then, suddenly, he began buying armor. He did not amass the largest armor collection in the country, but it is one of the finest, and it contains, most importantly, representative examples of various periods and places. It is obvious when you look at this collection that Mr. Walters was buying it to create one more department in his museum."

Another example is the small but fine collection of impressionist paintings. The American painter Mary Cassatt suggested to Mr. Walters that his collection should contain some impressionists to complement the other holdings in paintings, and he subsequently bought from her several of the impressionist works now in the collection.

To gain some understanding of the scope of the collections, it is necessary to turn to a Walters Gallery publication, which calls it, "One of the few remaining great collections gathered in the grand manner. Its incredible range and abundance give it the flavor of the vast hereditary collections of Europe. The too careful premeditation and weighing of responsibilities which necessarily must discipline the purchase of public museums have here not left their suffocating pressure...."

"There is found here material that is rarely accessible to the public in this country....One may draw attention to the importance of such groups as the ancient bronzes, the Etruscan and Phoenician objects, the Islamic pottery and metalwork, the early medieval jewelry, the Byzantine material, the Romanesque and Gothic ivories, the enamels, the large collection of illuminated manuscripts, the Renaissance bronzes, Sevres porcelains, incunabula and old bindings."

While Mr. Walters's gift of the gallery to Baltimore is the only one that is within the scope of our study, it should be noted that this remarkable man also gave Baltimore its system of public baths. In the years before everyone had bathrooms, these were used by about 250,000 people a year. And one cannot help mentioning some other gifts, as related in the Walters publication. In his will were:

"Large bequests to the Metropolitan Museum of Art, to Harvard, to Georgetown University, and [in Baltimore] the Family Welfare Association [a forerunner of the present Family and Children's Society]. During his lifetime, among other benefactions, he....was a liberal contributor to the endowment of the Johns Hopkins University, founded and endowed at its medical school the Department of Art as Applied to Medicine....erected the main building of Georgetown Preparatory School near Washington, was a generous friend of the Peabody Institute....presented the magnificent Lucas collection of sculpture, paintings and prints to the Maryland Institute, enriched the Metropolitan Museum of Art....with an extensive assemblage of Rembrandt etchings and with many other gifts...."

Like so many other collectors and benefactors (George Peabody, Enoch Pratt and Mrs. Jacobs, for instance), Mr. Walters was childless. He did not marry until 1922, when he wed the widow of E. Pembroke Jones. He had lived often with the Joneses for many years, at their homes in New York, Newport, Wilmington, North Carolina and Palm Beach. He did not really live in Baltimore, but maintained the house on Mount Vernon Place as his legal and voting residence.

A curious fact about the house, one which many people noticed, was that, although Mr. Walters was seldom in residence, the lantern in the vestibule was lighted night and day, 365 days a year. This became something of a mystery, and so the story grew up that it was a symbol of regret and hope. Henry Walters's sister, Jennie, married Warren Delano, and people said she and her father, William Walters had quarreled over the marriage and later Henry left the light burning in the vestibule in the hope that should Jenny ever seek a reconciliation and come to the house, it would be a signal of welcome to her. A nice romantic tale, but not true. Jennie stayed in the house many times, and as noted Mr. Delano was related to the architect of Henry Walters's gallery. (It is interesting to note that Mr. Walters's step-daughter, the daughter of Mrs. Jones, also married an architect, the same John Russell Pope who designed the addition to the Jacobs house next door at 7 West.) Besides, Henry was seldom in Baltimore, so Jenny would scarcely have sought him here.

Architect Francis Jencks, who grew up two doors away at One West, recalls that his mother was "in stitches when she heard the story of the vestibule light and Jennie Walters, because it was so absurd. What happened was that Mr. Walters complained so often and so loudly about inadequate lighting on Mount Vernon Place that finally the city fathers installed a light in his vestibule which was hooked up to the city gas line and which it cost him nothing to keep burning all the time."

On the other side of the Walters house from the Jacobs mansion is 3 West, which according to one source has a Walters connection. Built about 1850 (probably by Niernsee and Neilson) for John Nelson, Attorney General of Maryland, it was subsequently for a time a boarding house at which William Walters is supposed to have stayed before he bought 5 West. Other owners have included Joseph Wilkins, Mr. and Mrs. Thomas Poultney, William F. Burns, and the Patrick McEvoys. For a time it was Red Cross headquarters, and later the home of an educational establishment called Eastern College. It has in recent years been renovated as a group of attractive condominium apartments. Number 3 is thus one of a number of houses on the Place which had numerous owners and residents. Next door to it is a house which has had a quite different history, that of three ownerships in 130 years.

Number One West, one of the great houses of Mount Vernon Place and indeed one of the great townhouses of the Nineteenth Century, is known, by the names of all its owners, as the Thomas-Jencks-Gladding house. Designed by Niernsee and Neilson and erected in 1849, its architectural style has been variously named because there are aspects of more than one style. In form it is much like that of the earlier and more

William Walters as an old man. Looks as if he suspects something or someone, doesn't he?

The original Walters gallery, the 1885 addition to the back of the house at 5 West. It's easy to see that this gallery isn't going to be adequate for long.

The seated lion was one of the five Barye sculptures that William Walters gave to the city in 1885. It sits in the west square, looking rather sleepily at the monument.

The statue of Chief Justice Roger Brooke Taney was a gift to the city by William Walters. This is a copy of the original by William Henry Rinehart, which Walters gave to Annapolis. Rinehart was a sculptor discovered working in the Bevan marble yards where the Peabody Institute now stands, and sent to Rome to be educated. He remained in Rome and became one of the leading American classical sculptors of the third quarter of the Nineteenth Century. The Rinehart School of Sculpture at the Maryland Institute is named for him. Long out of favor, his works may be on the verge of a revival. One small marble piece recently brought $50,000 at an auction sale in Virginia, and went to well-known West Coast collectors.

The four groups, War, Peace, Force, and Order, by Barye, were also given by William Walters. Though they now reside on the ends of the balustrades to east and west of the monument, they were originally placed differently. Each group includes an animal; animals were Barye's chief claim to fame.

"Military Courage" by P. Dubois, in the west square, was another of William Walters's gifts.

The south square. As it appears that One West, left rear, still has an open porch on the back, this photo must date to before 1893. The fountain in the center of the walkway was called the "Lily Fountain".

The young Henry Walters was a handsome man with a firm jaw and a look of vision in his eyes. The Wall Street Journal, *which said he didn't have his picture taken between the ages of 4 and 60-odd, obviously didn't know about this one. The moustache seems to be an attempt to copy his father.*

Henry Walters with the woman he married at the age of 73. He had lived with Mr. and Mrs. E. Pembroke Jones for years, and when Mr. Jones died he married the widow. Is this a honeymoon photograph? She, at any rate, looks properly pleased.

34

This shot from a newspaper of about 1904 shows the four houses on the west side of South Washington Place where the Walters Art Gallery is now. They were nice houses, all built about the middle of the Nineteenth Century. The upper two became a boarding house in the Seventies and the Eighties, and Woodrow Wilson and Jerome Bonaparte the younger stayed there.

The Walters Art Gallery, original building, under construction between 1905 and 1909. The brick arches of the courtyard's first floor are complete, and the columns which will support the second floor arches are in place. It is said that the gallery is built over a stream, and that pilings driven to support it kept disappearing in quicksand until a system of anchoring them with barges was devised; and that thus the building actually floats.

The Walters Art Gallery's original building, by Delano and Aldrich, has a Renaissance facade which may be a little less pleasing than its interior courtyard. It is, however, unaggressive and of decent proportions and good scale.

The interior of the original Walters Art Gallery as it appears today. The courtyard, modeled on that of a Genoa palace, is a beautiful interior space.

typical Greek Revival house across the street, the Tiffany-Fisher house at 8 West. However its tall French windows with their surmounting brackets on the first two floors and its substantial modillioned cornice with iron palmettes suggest the Italianate style then coming into vogue. (Pictures from as early as the 1880's show it with shutters, though a view from 1850 shows it without; when the shutters, now gone, were added is not known.)

Especially impressive is the portico with its fluted columns and double stairway. When the Garrett house (now gone) at Cathedral and Monument Streets was erected a dozen years later, this portico was copied almost exactly.

The entrance leads to a marble-floored hall with Corinthian columns, at the rear of which a dramatic spiral staircase ascends to the second floor, culminating in a dome with a stained glass center.

Lavishly ornamented throughout, the house was built for John Hanson Thomas and his wife, the former Annie Campbell Gordon, who in 1850 were Society from 'way back. Dr. Thomas was descended from the John Hanson who was President of Congress under the Articles of Confederation after the Revolutionary War. Mrs. Thomas was a Virginia heiress of that Gordon clan which has already appeared in this account and will do so again.

The Thomases were fond of entertaining, and the house was certainly fitted to the purpose. To the right of the great hall is a 60-foot-long double parlor, also with Corinthian columns; on the other side of the house are two rooms which in the Thomases' day served as library and dining room. The library was done in Elizabethan Revival style, with mahogany woodwork containing the carved heads of 36 famous people including Dante, Cicero, Columbus, Queen Elizabeth, Shakespeare, and Benjamin Franklin. The Gothic Revival dining room was paneled in golden oak and had a brass-studded ceiling.

In these rooms Dr. and Mrs. Thomas entertained, among many others, the Prince of Wales before he became Edward VII and the Polish patriot Kossuth, who mentioned to Mrs. Thomas a confection he liked in Poland. She had her cook make it for him, and thus was born the Kossuth cake, which became a popular local dessert.

Dr. Thomas, doctor and subsequently banker, and his wife were Southern sympathizers during the Civil War, for which he paid by spending seven months during the early part of the war in Fort McHenry and other northern jails. Mrs. Thomas was first vice president of the Southern Relief Association after the war.

One of Dr. Thomas's sons, Douglas Thomas, was famous for his Madeira parties, and the following story is told about one of them:

Once Mr. Douglas Thomas asked several of his most discriminating friends to test their knowledge of his Madeira wines. All labels were covered; three bottles were from Mr. Thomas's cellar, the fourth he had bought from the corner grocer. After extensive tasting they all agreed on the superiority of one bottle, which to everyone's great surprise turned out to be the one from the corner grocer. The next morning Mr. Thomas hurried to the store to ask the grocer where he had obtained the mysterious bottle of

Madeira. "Why," the grocer replied, "your butler sold it to me. He said that you had given him one of your best wines as a reward for his faithful service."

Baltimore was a Madeira town in the Nineteenth Century. A great deal of the fortified wine, which is cousin to Port and Sherry but like neither, was imported from the island of Madeira, and some men developed extensive Madeira cellars of which they were quite proud. Some of the cellars were being sold off as recently as 20 years ago.

Anne Kinsolving Brown tells another story about Madeira tasting: "The Madeira Club, to whose dinners my father went, took itself very seriously. Members collected Madeira the way people collect paintings now, and there was a man named Charlie Fisher who was the Madeira taster. They would appoint a taster, and when the consignments came in the taster went down to the commission house and selected the Madeira for the members.

"Well, Charlie Fisher died in the course of time, and one year certain members proposed that they invite his 21-year-old son to a dinner. This was considered a great sacrilege by some, because they were all from 60 up. After dinner they brought the finger bowls in, with two Madeira glasses turned upside down in the water, and they rinsed them out after each vintage. So on this occasion Mr. Douglas Thomas went pompously to the sideboard and picked out a decanter of Madeira and brought it over and filled this boy's glass and said, 'Tell me what you think of this.'

"And the boy tasted it and said, 'It has a distinct taste of tar.'

"Well, everybody around the table gasped, and thought, that's what comes from asking this young whippersnapper to dinner. On the contrary, Mr. Thomas went over to the sideboard and brought back the little piece of paper that was always attached with the history, gave the boy a bear hug and said, 'My boy, you have your father's taste.' The cask of Madeira had been on a ship called the Anne McKim, which got caught in a storm, and to save the Madeira they had to put it in a coil of tarred rope, and it was pronounced to have definitely got the taste of tar in it. So you can't write off the young."

The elder Thomases, Dr. and Mrs. John H., died in 1881 and 1886, respectively. In 1892 One West was sold to Mr. and Mrs. Francis M. Jencks. Their son, architect Francis Jencks, says that his parents, who had lived in New York until then, moved to Baltimore primarily because his father wanted to live in One West.

The Jenckses hired Mrs. Jencks's brother, architect Charles A. Platt, to modernize the house. Mr. Platt added the bay window on the Washington Place side of the house to give more light to the dining room; enclosed the back porch to create a conservatory; widened the curving staircase to make it more graceful and substituted a Tiffany skylight for the original one at the top; removed woodwork and Victorian mantels and did the house over in the lighter, Italian Renaissance style fashionable in the 1890's.

During the Baltimore Fire of 1904 the Jenckses could see flames reflected in the windows of the Greenway house opposite. They packed up some of their possessions in the event it became necessary to leave. Many other residents of the Place did the same thing. D. K. Este Fisher wrote 70 years later, "When it looked as though the fire might come up to Mount Vernon Place, my great-grandmother Este, who lived with my grandparents [at 8 West] and was then 101 years old, was prepared to flee to my parents' house. . . . at Park Avenue and Lanvale Street, and for two days and nights the 'Victoria' and horses, and Augustus, the old black coachman, stood ready in the driveway."

In the event, no one had to leave; but shortly after the fire Mount Vernon Place became infested with rats from the burnt-out district, seeking new homes. The Jenckses and many other residents of the Place had to call in the ferreters.

Mr. Jencks, a civic leader, was a founder of Calvert School, and, as a board member of Johns Hopkins University, played a major role in moving the university to its Homewood campus. After his death in 1918 Mrs. Jencks continued to live at One West for 35 years. A member of the boards of Calvert School, the Union Memorial Hospital, and the Women's Civic League, she was also a founder of the Mount Vernon Club and the Flower Mart. During and after World War II she allowed some of the first-floor rooms to be used by the Red Cross, CARE, and the United Nations Association of Maryland, all rent-free. That was after the days of the Jenckses' major entertaining, when among the guests were Warren Harding and Mrs. Herbert Hoover.

After Mrs. Jencks died in 1953, the house's future was in doubt. Not wanting to see it destroyed, the city bought it for $75,000 in anticipation of the expansion of the Walters Art Gallery (about which more later). But the planned expansion did not take place on Mount Vernon Place, and the house remained vacant for 10 years. Still painted gray — most large brick houses of its period were painted to simulate stone — the paint at one point looked so bad that neighbors subscribed funds to have the brick cleaned. The brick has been exposed ever since, and in recent years there has been a fashion for removing paint from Nineteenth Century brick buildings. While the natural brick may be preferred today, it is not authentic. Number 8 West, of the same period, retains by contrast its painted exterior.

In 1962 Eastern College, which at that point occupied 3 West, offered to buy One West for the $75,000 the city had paid for it. But as the city was contemplating this offer Harry Lee Gladding, owner of an automobile firm, offered to pay $100,000. After a delay of some months, the city sold it to Mr. Gladding, who rehabilitated it functionally, restored many of its interior beauties, and furnished it in the style of Louis XV. It remained in his hands for 20 years, until in 1982 he decided to sell it.

The Thomas-Jencks-Gladding house's history has paralleled that of Mount Vernon Place: the home of the socially prominent in the Nineteenth Century and the early Twentieth, subsequent decline, threats to its architectural integrity, a successful preservation movement, and a renewal of interest in the area, which has produced rising property values. It is appropriate that One West should reflect this history, for it is constructed on the site of the first house on Mount Vernon Place, where its first resident lived. That, however, was no mansion but a modest building which was home to

Nicholas Hitzelberger, foreman of the stonecutters working on the Washington Monument between 1815 and 1829, and keeper of the monument.

During the construction of the monument, there was a marble yard on the site of the present Peabody Institute; it stretched down the east side of Washington Place to what is now Centre Street. It was called the Bevan yards, and there Hitzelberger worked on the marble that was brought in from Baltimore County to be cut for the column. As he lived just across the way his daughter Mary was frequently around the marble yard, and later remembered that one day Enrico Causici, who carved the statue of Washington atop the monument, sat her on the head when it was still on the ground, saying that one day she could say she had sat on Washington's head.

Hitzelberger died in 1833, just four years after the completion of the monument, but his daughter continued to live in the house near the monument for a time; her daughter, later Mrs. Virginia Anne Jones, was born there in 1837.

Although Mount Vernon Place was just beginning then, 1837 was in a sense the midpoint of the history of the land — about 150 years ago, and about 150 years after George Eager purchased the land from Lord Baltimore in 1688. It was part of a huge estate called Belvidere, roughly bounded by what are now Biddle Street on the north, Eutaw Street on the west, Jones Falls on the east, and stretching far south of what is now Mount Vernon Place. The estate passed to the original owner's son, John Eager, and then to his daughter Ruth, who married Cornelius Howard in 1738. It was their son, John Eager Howard, who became a general in the Revolutionary War, who subsequently gave the land for the Washington Monument, and whose equestrian statue is in the north square.

If you picture Baltimore in 1815, clustered around the harbor considerably to the south, it will seem strange that its people, having decided to erect a great monument to Washington, should decide to place it far out of town — as if, say, we were to decide to put up a monument to someone and place it several miles north of Towson. But there was a reason for that, and the reason takes us to the real beginning of our story, in 1809.

In that year a group of patriotic citizens formed a committee to build a monument to George Washington, then regarded almost as a god by the country he had "fathered" and served as its first President. An architectural competition was announced; among those submitting designs were Maximilian Godefroy, designer of the First Unitarian Church, and (though the submission was anonymous) probably Benjamin Latrobe, designer of Baltimore's greatest building, the first Roman Catholic Cathedral in the United States, now known as the Basilica of the Assumption. Latrobe, a friend of Thomas Jefferson, was also the first architect of the Capitol in Washington. But the competition was won by Robert Mills, from South Carolina — a surprise, as he submitted his design after the official closing date of the competition and his project for a colossal column was clearly the most costly to build. Nevertheless, the judges awarded him the commission.

The first proposed site of the monument was Court Square, where the Battle Monument by Godefroy now stands. But when the plans for the great column were announced, residents of the area near the square were afraid it might fall over on their houses. The solution was found when General Howard offered land on his estate for the site.

The cornerstone was laid on July 4, 1815, and the Washington statue by Causici raised to complete the monument on November 25, 1829. Mills's original conception was considerably more ornate than the finished product, with exterior balconies on several levels and between them inscriptions and other decorations. One by one these embellishments were discarded in an economy drive, for the monument even in its simplified form cost twice the estimated $100,000, far more than the proceeds of the lottery which was to pay for it. Most people today would say the simplifications in design were all to the good, for the monument is more forceful as it is.

Made of Cockeysville marble, it consists of a square base containing a room which surrounds the bottom of the column, and the plain column rising to the base of the statue representing Washington in the act of resigning his commission in the Continental Army at Annapolis in 1782. The monument is 178 feet high overall and can be ascended via an interior circular staircase of 228 steps. It does not seem so grand to our eyes as it did to those who watched the raising of the statue on that November day in 1829 — it was their Empire State Building, their World Trade Center, or perhaps more nearly their ascent of Everest, their flight to the moon, their great achievement hailed by Presidents and the country at large. It remains one of Baltimore's finest accomplishments, and one of the very few colossal columns built in modern times. It has been compared with the Colonne Vendome in Paris.

But the monument would not seem half so impressive, nor would the area have become half so desirable, without the four parks which form a Greek cross around it. General Howard gave only the land for the monument and that immediately around it, the small square paved in Belgian block at the center of Mount Vernon and Washington Places. It was his heirs (or perhaps the executors of his estate working for the heirs) who came up with the plan for the parks and pushed through the Maryland Legislature (the necessary route in those days) two pieces of legislation. The first altered the already-laid-out grid plan for the expansion of Baltimore to provide for the four parks. The second allowed the land adjacent to the parks to be sold in lots rather than in a single piece.

Thus was created a plan which benefited both the city and the Howard heirs, as the lots bordering the parks quickly rose in value. The first house, on the site of the present Mount Vernon Place Methodist Church northeast of the monument, was erected in 1829 by General Howard's son Charles, who married the daughter of Francis Scott Key, the author of the "Star Spangled Banner," who died in the house in 1843, an event memorialized by a plaque outside the church. An imposing Greek Revival mansion, the house was an act of faith for Howard. It was so far out of town at the time that his friends said he'd have to sell it as a beer garden. Virginia Anne Jones, granddaughter of Nicholas Hitzelberger, later noted that the Howard house "was quite in the country, with Howard's woods forming a dark mysterious forest as far to the north as the eye could reach." There was supposedly a duelling ground where the Stafford Hotel (now the Stafford Apartments) stands today.

Some say that the residents of the city were pushed north by the first great wave of immigration, between 1830 and 1850. Whatever the reason, building on Mount Vernon Place was slow in the 1830's but rapid in the 1840's. The next house to go up was on the corner northwest of the monument, where the Washington Apartments now stand. It was built about 1835 by Edward McDonald Greenway, Sr., one of Baltimore's first major art collectors. He, and then his son, and their families lived there for 70 years, until, just after the Baltimore Fire, the house was torn down for the apartment building.

Two doors west of the Greenway house is 8 West, one of the earliest houses on the squares and the oldest surviving building. Now the Mount Vernon Club, it is known in popular lore as the Tiffany-Fisher house.

In 1835 William Tiffany, a commission merchant, bought the first of two lots from George Howard (governor of Maryland from 1831 to 1833) for $2,625. He didn't build immediately and by 1841 had decided on a larger house than one lot would provide. In that year he bought the lot to the west of his (which would have been number 10 in the current numbering system, but the numbering was quite different originally) from General Benjamin C. Howard for $4,250. Land values were going up.

The house was completed, according to tax records, about 1842. (The late architect D. K. Este Fisher, descendant of subsequent owners of the building, stated in a 1972 letter that he had seen a plasterer's mark dated 1834 in the house; but as there is no other evidence for such a date, and considerable evidence for the later date, it is likely that either the plasterer or Mr. Fisher transposed the last two digits.)

There is some feeling that the house was designed by Niernsee before his partnership with Neilson, but no evidence. Another account says that the house is after the design of Mme. H. P. Lefevre's house in Franklin Street, which in turn was based on the house of Gustav Lurman in Hamburg, Germany. Whoever was responsible, the exterior is one of the treasures of Greek Revival architecture in America and my own favorite of all the buildings on Mount Vernon and Washington Places. Its simple, forceful Doric portico, its subtly tripartite division with the center slightly indented and only the central window pedimented, its dentiled cornice and gallery concealing two fourth-floor dormers, all add up to a triumph of refined understatement and elegant proportion, a rare survival of the very best period of Baltimore architecture and one of the happiest achievements of that characteristic Baltimore restraint which is so evident on Mount Vernon Place. Those who can appreciate this building no doubt understand the spirit which created it; those who love it no doubt share that spirit.

While most accounts give the first owner as William Tiffany, Mr. Fisher, in his 1972 letter, stated that the house was owned by "Henry Tiffany of Baltimore, who married in 1840 Sally Jones Milligan McLane (1820-1877), daughter of Louis McLane (1784-1857) of Washington, Delaware, and 'Bohemia,' Cecil County, Maryland (Congressman, Senator, Secretary of the Treasury, Secretary of State, Minister to England, President of the B. & O. Railroad)."

Mr. Tiffany, whether William or Henry, died in 1851; his children Elise and George lived at 8 West until 1859. During the Civil War the house was the home of the Allston Club (named for Washington Allston) until in 1863 the occupying Union Army closed it and arrested some of its members for plots against the North.

From 1865 to 1877 Miss S. A. Kummer's school for young ladies was operated there; subsequently the school moved to 122 West Franklin Street and became the Edgeworth School. Dr. and Mrs. Henry Hupfeld occupied 8 West for a decade beginning in 1877, and from 1889 to 1897 it was the home of Mr. and Mrs. Thomas Deford. Judge William A. Fisher moved in in 1898; he died in 1901, but his widow, her mother, his son William A. Fisher, Jr., and his daughter and son-in-law, Senator and Mrs. William Cabell Bruce, occupied the house until 1919.

The Fishers and Bruces, however, never owned the house. D. K. Este Fisher's letter records that, "At the turn of the century...the house was for sale, but there was a 'flaw in the title' and my grandfather [Judge Fisher] acquired it under a '99-year-lease.' " In fact, the ownership remained with the Tiffany family until 1875, and from then until 1897 it was owned first by Edna Solomon and then by Abigail S. Hupfeld. From 1897 to 1919, the years of the Fisher-Bruce tenancy, it was in the control of Edward M. Vickery, a trustee for the surviving heirs of Mrs. Hupfeld.

During the early years of the Fisher residence, the house was extensively "Georgianized" inside. The exterior remains virtually original, but the interior is considerably changed from its early appearance.

As Mr. Fisher's letter continues, "There was extensive remodeling under Mr. Randall, the architect, including much of the elaborate woodwork, the mantels, etc., and great mahogany doors....on the second floor, said to have been salvaged from a well-known house in New York...." In 1919, as Mr. Fisher continues, "the title was cleared and the property was acquired by Mr. and Mrs. Blanchard Randall."

There has been some confusion as to exactly when the house was altered, partly owing to the fact that the "Mr. Randall" whom Mr. Fisher names was Henry Randall, brother of Blanchard Randall. Other accounts also refer to alterations under the Blanchard Randalls. The preponderance of the evidence seems to suggest that in fact Judge Fisher did hire Henry Randall and it was at the turn of the century that the major alterations were carried out, though there were probably subsequent alterations under the Blanchard Randalls.

They lived there until 1941, at which time the house was sold to the Mount Vernon Town Club, which still owns it under the name of the Mount Vernon Club. It is a merger of two former clubs, the Mount Vernon, which had had quarters at 3 West, and the Town Club, which had had rooms at the Washington Apartments. They joined to buy 8 West, and have cared for the building very well for the last 40 years.

Despite or because of the alterations, the house is still beautiful inside. As in many houses of the period, the main reception rooms are on the second floor. The first floor contains a large parlor to the right of the central hall and a cloak room to the left. Farther back on the left an archway leads to a bold staircase lighted at its curve by an arched window. The second floor contains what were the library, the music room and the dining room. Here are the doors from New York, flanked by Corinthian pilasters and with broken pediments above (results of the Georgianizing). And here the floor-to-ceiling windows give great light to the high rooms. Above, on the third floor, are two guest bedrooms, in one of which the Duke and Duchess of Windsor stayed when they visited Baltimore in 1959.

The Tiffany-Fisher house is from a time when building was picking up considerably on the squares. An 1847 photograph shows the north side of the west square built up to number 14, which is under construction. An 1850 picture shows the south side of the square built except for numbers 3 and 11. And as long as we are on this square, a word about the other houses and their owners is in order.

On the north side number 6, just east of the Tiffany-Fisher house, was built sometime before 1847 by Lambert Gittings, and subsequently owned by O. F. Bresee and William F. Cochran. It was Mr. Cochran who built the Washington Apartments, to a Beaux Arts design by E. H. Glidden, in 1906. At some point in its history, probably in the 1890's, 6 West acquired a new facade. About that time a number of the houses on the square added fourth floors and changed facades. Number 6 is now the home of the English-Speaking Union.

Twelve West, on the other side of the Tiffany-Fisher house, was built by Alexander Gordon, thus giving the Gordon clan connection with the building of three houses on Mount Vernon Place. (Douglas Gordon, their descendant, claims this is more than were built by any other family. The Garretts, he says, "merely *owned* more houses, and anybody can do that.")

After the Gordons, the Hall Pleasantses lived at 12 West for many years. During the 1950's the Edgar Bermans, who had an extensive art collection, owned the house. Subsequently Mr. and Mrs. J. Harvey Kayne were in residence while the house still belonged to Dr. Berman. Recently it was on the market, and the real estate firm which was selling it claimed it to be the oldest surviving house on Mount Vernon Place, built in 1830. To my knowledge no one else has ever made such a claim about the house; it does not look like an 1830 house, and Douglas Gordon, great nephew of the first owners, disputes the claim.

Number 14 West was built by George Small originally, and owned by the Tiffany family for a time. But the best-known resident was Theodore Marburg, diplomat, ambassador to Belgium, and friend of Presidents. According to the present owners, Mr. Marburg bought the house in 1890 and over the next six years had it enlarged by one and a half stories and lavishly decorated inside. It was then that the house's severely plain facade was altered to the present one (according to architect Francis Jencks the architect of the alterations was Pleasants Pennington).

The Thomas-Jencks-Gladding house is basically a Greek Revival house with Italianate or Renaissance influences. It was originally painted gray, and at one time had shutters, though they were probably not original.

The original Mills design for the Washington Monument. It is easy to see how radically different this design was from the finished product, though the concept was the same. Not only did the balconies and the inscriptions on the shaft disappear, but so did the arch at the base and the four sculptures at the corners of the base. And in the execution the triumphal chariot at the top became the statue of Washington resigning his commission.

WASHINGTON MONUMENT AND HOWARD'S PARK. 1829.

In 1829 Robert Cary Long, Jr., son of an architect and himself to become the architect of such buildings as St. Alphonsus' Church and the Franklin Street Presbyterian Church, made this watercolor. It shows the new monument, the Howard house to the right, and at left under the trees the small house of Nicholas Hitzelberger.

This fine view of the monument, drawn by T.K. Wharton and engraved by James Smillie for the New York Mirror in 1835, is one not often seen. Looking from the west, Wharton shows that the monument was still outside of town (his strategically-placed tree to the left allows him to avoid showing the Howard house), but the town was creeping toward the hill. To the right we see buildings advancing north on Charles Street, and the dome of Godefroy's First Unitarian Church. This is an especially interesting view, as it shows the topography from the west, with a ravine where the present Centre Street cuts through from west to east.

48

A ca. 1840 view of the monument with the Howard house to the right and the Greenway house to the left. Not an astounding view, but rarely if ever published, and it shows the extent of the very large Howard house. The fence has gone up around the monument.

Enrico Causici's statue of Washington atop the monument is rarely seen up close. Whether because of the effects of time and weather or because Causici did it that way, the statue looks little like most portraits of Washington. In fact, it looks like James Cagney.

This Sachse chromo-lithograph from the 1850's is a complement to the aerial views from the north that Sachse printed between 1850 and 1874. Here we are looking up from the south and see the Howard house facing us on the right, the Greenway house facing us on the left, the back of One West and the four houses to the corner of Centre Street (where the Walters Art Gallery is now) on the left, and the five houses on the east side of South Washington Place on the right. Construction of the Peabody Institute has not begun, and we can see the small building that was headquarters for the Bevan marble yards when the monument was being built. There seems to be a house to the east of the Howard house, perhaps what is now 10 or 12 East.

VIEW OF BALTIMORE CITY, MD

FROM THE NORTH

E. Sachse and Co., a well-known Baltimore lithographer of the Nineteenth Century, published three aerial views of Baltimore from the north, with Mount Vernon Place in the foreground: the first in 1850, the second in 1862 and the third in 1874. We have chosen to include the middle one. By 1862, 3 West and 11 West, not included in the 1850 view, have been built, as has the Garrett house on the southwest corner of Cathedral and Monument Streets. By 1862, also, the first three bays of the Peabody building seem completed (though the Institute was not to open until 1868), replacing the marble yard which had occupied the space since the building of the Washington Monument. On the near side of East Mount Vernon Place the Howard house is still at the corner of Washington Place. By 1874 the Mount Vernon Place Methodist Church will have replaced it. Those with a magnifying glass will be able to make out many familiar Baltimore landmarks in the background of this picture, including St. Vincent de Paul Church, the Shot Tower, the First Unitarian Church and Latrobe's Cathedral, now the Basilica of the Assumption.

The Tiffany-Fisher house, at 8 West, is the finest example of Greek Revival domestic townhouse architecture left in Baltimore.

Mr. and Mrs. Theodore Marburg, on board ship. Mr. Marburg's glasses are the perfect touch for that face.

An interior of the library in the Marburg house, 14 West, shows the confused splendor in which the Marburgs lived. The French writing table, ihe bookcase, the huge-patterned wallpaper, the rocking chair, the chandelier, and all the rest do not seem to go together to our eyes; but they were quite something 50 years ago.

This photo of the north side of the west square may not have been published since the 1920's, when it was included in Letitia Stockett's Baltimore: A Not-Too-Serious History. *Taken between 1885 and 1895, it shows the Walters sculptures in place (dedicated in 1885) and the eastern corner of 18 West, torn down for the 1895 Severn Apartments. It is also about the best picture we have of the Greenway house with a two-story building (presumably part of the Greenway house) between the main part of it and Number 6 West. It's also interesting that 14 West has not yet got its new facade, acquired in the Nineties.*

The south side of the west square today. Because the Garrett-Jacobs house is the largest mansion on any of the squares, because the Walterses lived next door, and because One West is one of the finest townhouses of the Nineteenth Century, this block has acquired more history than any of the others on Mount Vernon and Washington Places.

The north side of the west square today. The Tiffany-Fisher house, the lowest facade, is the oldest building left on any of the squares. Number 6, to the right of it, and Number 14, two doors to the left, got new facades and extra storys in the 1890's. The records on 16 West say that it was "built" in 1887, but there may have been an earlier house which was replaced or altered then. The Severn went up in 1895, along with the Stafford alarmed the residents about the height of buildings, and led to the first zoning law covering the squares.

Mr. Marburg entertained Presidents William Howard Taft and Woodrow Wilson at 14 West, and it is thought that the first draft covenant of the League of Nations was drawn up at the house, by Wilson and Mr. Marburg, working at a desk which is still there. Mr. Marburg died in 1941, and 15 years later his son sold the house to Dr. Charles Iliff. Since then it has been used for ophthalmologists' offices, but Dr. Iliff and his son, Dr. Nicholas Iliff, have done a fine job of preserving as much as possible of the interior decoration, especially that of the principal second floor reception rooms, and the fine plasterwork and woodwork of the grand staircase and the first floor front hall.

Next door, 16 West was designed by Joseph Evans Sperry for Edmund Didier in 1887, and owned successively by Alexander Winchester, Alexander Brown and David Bartlett. Mrs. Bartlett used to have her carriage brought around every Sunday morning for the drive to Grace and St. Peter's Church, a block away.

Where the Severn Apartments have stood since 1895, on the corner of Mount Vernon Place and Cathedral Street, there was formerly a house built by Chancellor Johnson, brother of United States Senator Reverdy Johnson, who also served as United States Attorney General and Ambassador to the Court of St. James's. The house was later lived in by the father of Henry White, who became Ambassador to France.

Across the street, number 15 West was built in three stages. First came the first three floors, two rooms deep (this before 1850). Next, at some unknown date, the back part of the house, beginning at the projecting bay on the Cathedral Street side. Finally, in the 1890's, the fourth floor. The house is an interesting one to look at, for these divisions are quite plain.

The owners of the land, and subsequently the house, have included James Howard McHenry, Edward Greenway (who built across the street), Robert Campbell, Zenus Barnum (relative of David Barnum, owner of the well-known Barnum's Hotel), Andrew M. Reid (director of the Mercantile Safe Deposit and Trust Company and partner in a wholesale grocery business, who resided there from 1872 to 1899), Alexander Shaw, Oscar Turner, Evalyn S. France (wife of Joseph I. France), and Georgia Gelston Jones. From 1929 to 1942 it was leased to the Women's City Club of Baltimore, a Democratic civic organization. Subsequently John and Lucille Matthews owned it for about 30 years, until in the 1970's it was sold to builder Joseph Azola. He soon sold it to the present owners, Vernon J. and Shirley Wiesand. Mrs. Wiesand has thoroughly researched the house's history.

Next door, 13 West was built sometime before 1850 and owned by a Mr. and Mrs. Parry and by James Hooper before it belonged to the Henry Pratt Janeses, he of the lawsuit against the nextdoor vestibule. It subsequently came into the hands of Mrs. Jacobs.

That, then, completes a tour of the west square. Across the way, the marble yard southeast of the Monument, where the Peabody Institute now stands, has been mentioned. Next to it, going down the hill on East Mount Vernon Place, were (before the Peabody) the houses of architect Josias Pennington and politician and writer John Pendleton Kennedy. It was in the Kennedy house that William Makepeace Thackeray, on his visit to Baltimore, was fed terrapin and wild duck and proclaimed both superb. Kennedy, author of *Swallow Barn* (published in 1832) and *Rob of the Bowl,* and friend of Washington Irving, was also at various times a Congressman from Maryland, Speaker of the Maryland House of Delegates, and Secretary of the Navy under President Millard Fillmore. With all that activity, he also managed to be a close friend of George Peabody and one of the prime movers in the establishment of the Peabody Institute.

George Peabody's gift to the city of Baltimore was important both for what it was and for what it started. One of the first great philanthropic gestures in America, it inspired many others, including, in Baltimore, those of Johns Hopkins, Enoch Pratt and William and Henry Walters.

The Peabody's donor neither was born in Baltimore nor lived most of his life here. He came from Danvers (now Peabody), Massachusetts, by way of Georgetown, just after the War of 1812. During the war, as an Army enlistee, he had met Baltimore merchant Elisha Riggs, and in 1815 joined him in setting up a dry goods firm here named Riggs, Peabody & Company. At that time, Mr. Peabody was 20 years old.

Like many others of his time, Mr. Peabody had come to Baltimore to make his fortune. The fastest-growing city in the nation, Baltimore's burgeoning port and strategic location between North and South combined to make it a leading commercial center in the first part of the Nineteenth Century. But it took a person of energy and business acumen to flourish in the competitive atmosphere, and Mr. Peabody had both. By 1829 the firm had offices in Philadelphia and New York, and its name, significantly, had been changed to Peabody, Riggs & Co.

Such a business, though it made him wealthy, was far too small a pond for Mr. Peabody. It was as a financier that he made the bulk of his huge fortune, and by the mid-1830's he had become convinced that the best place to be, if you were a financier, was London. So he moved there in 1837, never to return to Baltimore to live.

He didn't forget the city, though, or the friends he had made here; and in particular he didn't forget what it didn't have. Though a thriving commercial and industrial center, the Baltimore of that time was virtually bereft of any scholarly or artistic activity. As a son of Massachusetts, with its high intellectual traditions, Mr. Peabody couldn't help but notice how culturally deprived Baltimore was; and when he embarked on his extraordinary career as a philanthropist it was that deprivation that he was determined to remedy.

The Peabody Institute, it must be noted, was only one of Mr. Peabody's good works. In London, he built scores of thousands of housing units for the working class. For that charity he was offered a baronetcy by Queen Victoria, but would accept only a letter of thanks from Her Majesty. During the Civil War, he rescued, on the basis both of his immense fortune and of his known integrity, the faltering credit of the United States Government in England. It would take pages to relate the number and scope of his gifts to Harvard, Yale, Phillips Academy, Danvers, and others, including $2,000,000 for education in the South after the Civil War. But of all of them probably the best known today is the Peabody Institute.

For some years in the late 1840's and 1850's Mr. Peabody thought of founding a cultural institution in Baltimore. And he formally proposed it in 1857, in a letter to 25 of the city's leading citizens, who were to become the first board of trustees.

The founding letter showed that Mr. Peabody's ideas were thoroughly thought out and quite specific. He wished to endow an institution which would be at once a haven for the scholar and of use to the general public. He wanted, as the opening sentence of his letter said, "to establish and endow an Institute...which...may become useful towards the improvement of the moral and intellectual culture of the inhabitants of Baltimore, and collaterally to those of the State; and also, towards the enlargement and diffusion of a taste for the Fine Arts." To this end, he at first proposed to give something like $100,000 as seed money for the Institute, the rest to be raised in Baltimore. But his friend and adviser J. P. Kennedy, who apparently knew Baltimoreans better than Mr. Peabody did, wrote to him that the Institute would never become a reality if it had to be funded locally. And so Mr. Peabody ended up giving $1,400,000, an enormous sum for those days.

The Institute, Mr. Peabody's letter went on, was to have four separate but complementary departments: A library, a scholarly lecture series, an academy of music, and an art gallery. If that seems a large order for one institution, remember that Mr. Peabody was seeking to remedy Baltimore's lack of cultural life, and Baltimore in 1857 had none of those things.

The lecture series was to compensate for the fact that the city had no university. The library was because Baltimore had no public library (and the few special libraries were limited in scope and served members or subscribers only). The art gallery was because Baltimore had no museum or gallery with a major and permanent collection. And the music "academy" was because there was no music school (or at least none of any importance) here and furthermore there were no professional music organizations worthy of the name based in the city. Baltimore was a cultural desert, when compared with the other large cities of the northeast with which it was comparable in population and commercial and industrial importance.

The opening of the Institute was delayed until after the Civil War, but by 1862 the first three bays of the main building were completed to a somewhat free Renaissance design by Edmund G. Lind (the funny Palladianesque windows have always struck me as misconceived, but as a whole it is a handsome structure); and in 1878 the rest of the building was finished. This later part contains the magnificent library, one of the two or three finest interior spaces in Baltimore, which was designed by the institute's first provost and the man who more than any other was responsible for the Peabody's great collection of books, Nathaniel Holmes Morison.

The idea of a collection primarily for the scholar, but which could be used by any citizen, had been Mr. Peabody's. Mr. Morison carried out the founder's wishes by purchasing, in the United States and abroad, some 300,000 volumes which included the best works available in virtually every field of the arts and sciences. His grandson, historian Samuel Eliot Morison, later said that, "A wholesale book dealer in Paris, to whom I was introduced some 20 years after the Provost's death, told me that he had never known anyone, in Europe or America, who ordered books with such taste and discrimination as Dr. Morison." The result was a library which in some fields surpassed even the Library of Congress at the time, and which today contains some of the rarest books in the world.

Little need be said here about the conservatory, except that it soon became one of the finest in the country, a status which it enjoys to this day. The lecture series which Mr. Peabody envisaged lasted for half a century, and the art collection was, with the exception of the Walterses', the best that Baltimore had to boast in the late Nineteenth Century. An added important distinction was that Peabody's gifts were for the enjoyment of an unrestricted public.

In short, Mr. Peabody's attempt to make Baltimore intellectually respectable was a resounding success. Although the lectureship was terminated once Johns Hopkins University became well established, Mr. Peabody's gift was one of the principal stimuli which led Mr. Hopkins to establish his university. The art gallery which the Peabody opened was to be superseded by the Walters Art Gallery and later the Baltimore Museum, but Mr. Peabody's gift promoted the collecting fervor which led to those institutions; and parts of the Peabody collection now reside in both of them. Not only is the conservatory an important cultural jewel in itself; it was also the presence of the conservatory here which led directly or indirectly to most of the city's subsequently-formed professional musical bodies, including in particular the Baltimore Symphony Orchestra, the founders of which included many Peabody names and the membership of which to this day includes both graduates and faculty members of the Peabody. And if the Peabody library was later outdistanced in the size of its collection by the libraries of Hopkins and the Enoch Pratt, the existence and success of both those institutions can be traced back to the great room on Mount Vernon Place.

Mr. Peabody's gift was a direct inspiration to Enoch Pratt in founding one of the pioneer public libraries in the United States. And the existence of the Peabody library with its impeccable scholarly collection encouraged many of the professors who built Hopkins's international reputation to come to the university in the first place. They came because even though Hopkins in the early years had almost no library of its own they knew that at the Peabody they would find the resources they needed.

It is only fitting that when in the 1960's the Peabody found it could no longer afford the library, it was turned over to the Enoch Pratt Free Library, which for 16 years not only administered it but preserved and restored both building and collection. It is fitting that when the conservatory ran into financial difficulties in the 1970's it was taken into affiliation with Johns Hopkins University; Hopkins has also recently taken over the library, so the entire Peabody complex is now under one administration.

The Institute now owns the entire square block bounded by South Washington and East Mount Vernon Places, Centre and St. Paul Streets. As such it owns the five town houses on the east side of South Washington Place, opposite the Walters Gallery. In the corner one lived the Thomas Morrises in the Nineteenth Century, and it was Mrs. Morris who in the "season" of 1869-1870 introduced the custom of afternoon tea to Baltimore social circles. Other residents of those houses included the John Duers, who built 609; Richard Gittings; James H. Merrill, who invented the Merrill Carbine and personally persuaded the Czar of Russia to buy it for the Russian Army; and Mrs. Walter W. Abell.

The Peabody also owns the four houses on the south side of East Mount Vernon Place, from Leakin Hall, the Institute's preparatory building (completed in 1926) to the corner of St. Paul Street. All four of them, Numbers 27 through 33 East, are principally interesting for owners who never lived in them. They were once the property of the Caton sisters. The granddaughters of Charles Carroll of Carrollton, three of the Caton sisters electrified England with their beauty in the early Nineteenth Century, prompting King George IV to say that Baltimore was the place of origin of great beauties. They became known as the "Three Graces."

They did well in the marriage market. One secured the Marquess of Wellesley, brother of the Duke of Wellington. Another married the Duke of Leeds, and the third, Baron Stafford. Their less-beautiful sister Emily stayed in Baltimore and married John McTavish, British consul here. I have often wondered what their grandfather, one of the most distinguished signers of the Declaration of Independence, thought when all four of his granddaughters ended up married to Englishmen, three of them members of the House of Lords; for old Charles was still alive when they married.

The "Three Graces" never lived in the houses on East Mount Vernon Place, but rented them to such people as Robert McLane, later Governor of Maryland and Minister to France; George William Brown, who served on the boards of the Peabody and Johns Hopkins but is remembered chiefly as the mayor of Baltimore who on April 19, 1861, "deemed it his duty," as Douglas Gordon has written, "to lead a Massachusetts regiment through the city in an unsuccessful attempt to maintain order and preserve life, though he was a Southern sympathizer." Every schoolboy knows that on that day in Baltimore the first blood of the Civil War was spilt.

Other, later residents of the houses included A. S. Abell, founder of the *Sunpapers;* Charles J. M. Gwinn, Attorney General of Maryland and the lawyer who drew the will of Johns Hopkins; Matilda Johnson, daughter of Senator Reverdy Johnson (whose brother Chancellor, you will remember, owned a house on the west square); former Mayor of Baltimore James H. Preston; and the W. Hall Harrises, Sr. and Jr., in this century. It is one of these houses which is supposed to have been a house of prostitution in the 1940's, when Mount Vernon Place was probably at its lowest ebb.

The north side of East Mount Vernon Place has the only example of speculative rowhouse building on the four squares. The six brownstones, numbers 18 to 28 East, were built by Richard E. France, known as the "lottery king" in the Nineteenth Century. He bought the six tracts of land from William Key Howard and built the brownstones during the Civil War. They were all sold before they were finished.

Albert Schumacher, a local businessman, built the impressive brownstone at 10 East in about 1850. The architects were our old friends Niernsee and Neilson. The house is of an Italianate Renaissance design, somewhat patterned after houses of the English architect Sir John Barry. The interior, altered in the 1890's, is chiefly notable for its second-floor front room, with the bay. Here there is elaborate woodwork, and a vaulted ceiling which rises to a painting of Aurora, goddess of the dawn, after Guido Reni. The house was later owned by the Von Lingen family, one of whom was German consul in Baltimore, and subsequently from 1901 to 1956 by Mr. and Mrs. John Rieman. Even in her last days there Mrs. Rieman, then a widow, employed a staff of seven servants. It is now owned by Mount Vernon Place Methodist Church, next door, which uses it for offices and the pastor's residence.

Other notable dwellers on the east square have included Charles J. M. Eaton, president of the Peabody board; the Misses Bond, who ran a most exclusive school for young ladies; Colonel Charles Carroll; and Mrs. Edgeworth Bird, in whose house Sidney Lanier gave poetry readings. In number 12 East lived American composer Hugh Newsom for many years before his recent death. It is not known whether during Mr. Newsom's tenancy, but at one time the great Polish pianist Jan Paderewski visited there, and there is a picture of him seated in the garden, composing.

Erected in 1873 to a design by the Baltimore firm of Dixon and Carson, the wonderfully exuberant Gothic pile that is the Mount Vernon Place Methodist Church occupies the site of Charles Howard's house. The church's polychromatic effect is achieved by green serpentine marble from Baltimore County and buff and red sandstone trim. The principal exterior features are the three spires and the large relieving arch enclosing the rose window. A mystery surrounds the row of faces carved in stone above the windows on the west front. They are said to be representations of prominent citizens of 1870, but no one can now identify them.

Behind the church, in the 700 block of Washington Place, lived at one time the Thomas Lanahans, who added the stone facade and fourth floor to number 717; Maurice Gregg and his mother, on the corner; Joshua and Francis Harvey, Horatio Whitridge, the T. Harrison Garretts and Eugene H. Beer.

Across the street, the fascinating chateauesque house on the corner was built by George Graham in 1893. His daughter, Isabella Graham, who made her debut in 1908, subsequently married a man named Hughes and moved away for a few years. But the marriage didn't last long, and she moved back into the house and lived there until the 1970's; that 80-year record of ownership is probably the longest by any one family on any of the four squares.

Next door, Dr. William A. Moale tore down his own house to erect the Stafford Hotel (now an apartment house), which opened in 1894. The following year the Severn Apartments went up, and the residents began to fear that too many tall buildings would ruin the scale of the four squares (as indeed they would have).

George Peabody, by William Wetmore Story, sits in the West square. The statue was presented to the city in 1890 by Robert Garrett, former president of the B. & O., who lived at 9-11 West.

In 1869 George Peabody visited his new institute and addressed Baltimore's school children on the front steps. At that point only the first three bays of the building were finished, and the John Pendleton Kennedy house is at the left. Peabody's head is in circle.

The first section of the Peabody building was completed in the early 1860's, only three bays wide on the Mount Vernon Place or main facade. In 1878 the rest of the building was completed to the design by Lind. The parts are so well integrated that one would never know from the outside that they are essentially separate buildings.

The interior of the Peabody Library shortly after it was opened, from the Provost's report for 1879. This lofty, grand, inspiring space was conceived by a man, Nathaniel Morison, who loved scholarship, for others who loved as he did. And for it and them he collected one of the finest libraries in the world, which still resides there. This is one of the greatest interiors in Baltimore, and invariably summons a gasp from those who see it for the first time. I am always amazed at the number of Baltimoreans who have never been inside the Peabody Library.

The southern half of the east side of South Washington Place contains a row of townhouses built about 1850 and now owned by the Peabody Institute. Except for the Schapiro house, which has the elaborate iron work, they are probably the least interesting houses on any of the four squares. The Schapiro house, built by Duers and once owned by Abells, has the sort of cast iron work that one used to see on a good number of Baltimore houses. Most of it has disappeared.

The four houses at the east end of the south side of East Mount Vernon Place, once owned by the Caton sisters, have had a curious history. Their most famous owners never lived in them, and perhaps never saw them. They were the home of at least two mayors of Baltimore and the founder of the Sunpapers, *but one was also a brothel for a while; and they have been vacant for two decades. The Peabody, which now owns them, has twice tried to tear them down, but each time preservationists have foiled the attempt. The Peabody now claims to have seen the light, and wants, it says, to convert them for institute use. Let's hope so.*

The brownstone row on the north side of the east square, built during the Civil War. This photo was taken about 10 years ago; some of the facades have deteriorated since then.

Asbury House, 10 East, was built in the 1850's to a design by Niernsee and Neilson. Its Italian Renaissance facade with rusticated stone at the first-floor level is really quite handsome. Unfortunately in recent years the brownstone has been covered with some sort of protective paint, so one no longer sees the stone itself.

This photograph of the north square can be dated 1904-1905. The Belvedere Hotel, in the right background, was completed in 1904 and the Greenway house, in the left foreground, was torn down for the Washington Apartments in 1905. Here we see how the top of the Stafford Hotel looked before it was altered a few years ago, and how the square looked before the re-landscaping of 1916. The statues of Roger Brooke Taney and John Eager Howard were in about the same positions they now occupy.

Mount Vernon Place Methodist Church, 1870, by Dixon and Carson, replaced the Charles Howard house northeast of the monument. The exuberant Gothic exterior is deplored by some as a detraction from the monument, but I think its presence adds an appropriate but not stodgy Victorian note to the squares. The architects kept their principal tower shorter than the monument as an act of deference.

Accordingly the Municipal Art Society (a forerunner of the Mount Vernon Improvement Association and other groups which have sprung up to preserve the integrity of the squares) went to the Maryland Legislature and in 1904 got a law passed limiting the height of the buildings on the four squares to no more than 70 feet above the base of the Washington Monument at street level.

This law was immediately challenged by William Cochran, who was in the process of tearing down the Greenway house to build the Washington Apartments, which he wanted to make taller than 70 feet. The case went all the way to the Court of Appeals, which upheld it in an interesting and essentially devious judgment. The height restriction had clearly been for aesthetic purposes, since because of the way the law read a building at the bottom of Washington Place could be a great deal taller than one at the top of the hill and still not exceed the statutory 70 feet above the base of the monument. But zoning restrictions for aesthetic reasons have always been subject to repeal in the courts. So the court, citing the recent Baltimore fire, judged that the restriction was for fire prevention purposes; and rationalized that the "base of the monument" wording was included because it would be easy for fire trucks, standing at the top of the hill, to direct their streams of water into the top floors of buildings at the bottom of the hill! At any rate, the law survives to this day, and to this day has limited the height of buildings on the four squares. It is surely one of the most effective zoning laws ever passed. (Mr. Cochran, defeated, saw to it that the Washington Apartments rose to a height of 69 feet, 8 inches; the building's height thus serves as a criterion for any building on Mount Vernon and Washington Places.)

While the Stafford was judged too tall, and ugly as well, it was certainly not ostracized. From its earliest days it was the place where many socially prominent newlyweds spent their wedding nights, and where their parents with estates in the rolling valleys north of Baltimore spent whole weeks at a time during the winter, or even the whole social "season."

What they looked out on from their windows was not what we see today, but it was a considerable improvement over the appearance of the squares in their earliest days. Washington Place is 150 feet wide by 744 feet long and Mount Vernon Place is 200 feet wide by 700 feet long. When the squares were first taking shape, the plots in them were little more than dirt rectangles where boys played games.

In the earliest days the south square was most popular for picking eggs, spinning tops and playing marbles. Then it was the west square for bandy, a game played with curved sticks of dogwood from the woods north of Madison Street. Still later it was the north square for townball, a forerunner of baseball.

About 1850 the squares were fenced in, but in the 1880's the fences were removed, the parks landscaped, and the Barye bronzes and some of the other sculptures added. Walkways enclosed circular and semicircular plots of grass. Robert Garrett donated the fountain in the west square (its shape and size, but not its sculpture, modeled after a fountain on the Champs-Elysees in Paris); the fountain in the east square was added later, and much later, in 1962, the naiad by Grace Turnbull was added to it.

Then came the day of the promenade. At the turn of the century dinner was at 2 on Sundays, and between church and dinner all the best people (and others who came to look at them) walked from lower Charles Street to Mount Vernon Place. "The Carrolls," wrote one reporter, "stopped to chat with the Keysers, the Manlys said hello to the Brents, the Garretts locked arms with the Gilmors," and all basked in the warm glow of their own superiority.

Easter Sunday, of course, was the biggest parade of all, and the parade on Easter of 1913 was particularly brilliant. In the midst of it, standing out even in that group, was a little man with a mustache and goatee, indelibly dapper in frock coat, pink tie, boutonnière of lilies-of-the-valley, and mouse-colored spats. Before ambling down Charles Street in the direction of Mount Vernon Place he paused for a time at the corner of Charles and Mulberry Streets, just up from his house on St. Paul Place. His one hand held that of a little niece, his other that of a little nephew. Shortly the two children's patience gave out, and one of them tugged at his hand and asked, "Uncle Walter, what are we standing here for?"

And Walter de Curzon Poultney, in his answer, summed up so much of what the social elite of his day, in Baltimore and elsewhere, thought of themselves. They were standing there, he said, "To take the air, my dears, and to give the people pleasure."

It was a statement entirely in character for Mr. Poultney. "Sir Walter," as he was referred to, never lived on Mount Vernon Place, but he was so much a part of its life, and so typified the residents' attitude of natural superiority that he should be included in any history of it.

He was one of the two famous bachelors of his generation and literally a member of the first family of the city, being descended from the first colonist born in what is now Baltimore.

He was a small man, and they say it was something to see him at dances, trippingly guiding some taller matron across the floor. Douglas Gordon recalls that, "he loved to dance with my mother, who was at least a head taller, and it was quite a sight to see them, she towering over him with an utterly serene expression on her face."

Although the newspapers from time to time referred to Mr. Poultney as a sort of arbiter elegantiarum of Baltimore, in reality he was more of a figure of fun to society. He was called "The White Rabbit", and he must have had some sense of humor about it because he once went to a fancy dress ball as a white rabbit.

But one joke got to him. At the New Year's Eve ball of the Bachelors Cotillon in 1901, Mr. Poultney was walking briskly down the sidelines when Ral Parr, dancing by, stuck out his leg and sent Mr. Poultney sprawling head over dignity. Attempting to get up, the unfortunate little man bumped into somebody else and went down for the second time. When he finally got up, he was so infuriated that he sought out Mr. Parr then and there and told him to his face that he was not a gentleman.

Mr. Poultney subsequently wrote to the Cotillon committee, and when the incident leaked out — it was something of a minor scandal — the papers reported that he had asked for Mr. Parr's resignation. But Mr. Poultney wrote a letter of correction about that: he had merely asked for a public apology, he said, and got it.

That seems to have been the largest ripple in Mr. Poultney's otherwise uneventful life; his daily activities may seem unremarkable, but they were regularly reported in the newspapers. A veteran traveler, he filled his house with objets d'art bought on his trips, and also brought back stories of having been feted everywhere. In 1898 he was entertained at Glamis Castle in Scotland by Lady Strathmore, and later when her daughter married he sent a present and got back a nice thank-you note from the girl, who is now Elizabeth the Queen Mother.

On one trip abroad he bought a Tyrolean walking costume, of the sort that shows one's knees between the short pants and the stockings. A photograph of him in this garb filtered back to Baltimore, and caused quite a sensation. When he returned he was asked if he intended to wear the costume in Baltimore. He replied that he might wear it in Philadelphia, implying that it was too bold for Baltimore.

Mr. Poultney managed to die, at the age of 84, in September of 1929, just before the stock market crash. He went at the right time, and in fact died within a few months of Baltimore's other famous man-about-town of his generation, Harry Lehr.

At the turn of the century, there were three ways into Society: blood, money, or the quality of being amusing. Society in those days was so dull that a few people with a certain flair and an ability to entertain ladies in an unthreatening way made it to the inner circles with no other qualifications whatever. Harry Lehr was one of them. He made a life of leisure bearable.

The son of a German merchant, Harry Symes Lehr first came to prominence in Baltimore when he appeared in a Paint and Powder Show in 1895 and during a chorus took and held a high falsetto note. Whether he planned it or not, he awoke the next morning to find that people were talking about him.

Not one to let an opportunity pass, Harry saw to it that he stayed in the public consciousness. He appeared at St. Ignatius Church one Sunday morning wearing a bracelet. A few weeks later he was seen sitting in a brougham on Lexington Street, knitting. And then one night after a ball Louise Morris, one of the celebrated Baltimore belles of the Nineties, dared him to walk through one of the fountains in Mount Vernon Place, and he did. What's more, he took her with him, evening dress and all.

Harry was a sensation! He had made Society sit up and take notice. But Baltimore Society was too small an arena for him. Through Mrs. Elisha Dyer he got himself introduced into Newport Society, and there, in that bastion of extravagant vulgarity, Harry found his natural home.

He gave a dinner party for Prince del Drago; the prince turned out to be a monkey which sat at table and amused itself by throwing champagne glasses at the other guests. The other guests loved it.

Harry walked down the street one morning talking baby talk to a rag doll, and everyone thought that was a scream. When one of the Newport Ladies told him to "run along" as "you are too ladylike for me" he replied "I wish I could say the same for you" and was acclaimed as a wit.

He did have a certain aptitude for putting people down. When a lady one evening bored a dinner table with her incessant talk about horses, Harry waited until she finally ran down and said to no one in particular, "A horse. A horse is an oblong animal with four legs, one at each corner."

By 1900 Harry had attained his desire. He was the social secretary to Mrs. John Jacob Astor. The power of such a position may be suggested by relating that Harry's predecessor, Ward McAllister, made up the guest list for Mrs. Astor's parties; the ballroom in the Astor mansion could hold 400, and those whom Mr. McAllister put on Mrs. Astor's guest list became New York's famous "the 400."

In Harry Lehr's time, he performed an act of kindness by persuading Mrs. Astor to wave her fan at Mrs. Gould at the opera one night. Mrs. Gould had been an actress before she married Mr. Gould, and no one was quite sure whether to accept her. Mrs. Astor's wave meant it was all right for Mrs. Gould to be sent invitations.

Harry was hired by a wine importer, and paid $40,000 a year simply to give parties and introduce the wine of the importer to his guests.

But just as he was at the crest, Harry, it would seem in retrospect, made a mistake. He got married. A bachelor may easily be the darling of society. It is not so easy for a married man. In 1901 Harry married a Drexel heiress, Elizabeth Drexel Dahlgren, whose first husband had died some time before.

They spent their wedding night — guess where? — at the Stafford Hotel on Washington Place; and it was one of the strangest wedding nights ever spent, there or anywhere. Years later, Mrs. Lehr wrote a book, and into it she put this account of that night:

Mrs. Lehr ordered supper to be served in her room. When it came she sent for the bridegroom. He failed to appear, and sent a maid back with a message that he would dine alone. She demanded that he appear. He appeared, and told her to her face that he had married her only for her money (the story was that he got an allowance of $25,000 a year), that he could not stand the sight of her, and that while he intended to observe the pleasantries in public theirs would be a marriage in name only.

It must be one of the longest such marriages in history, for it lasted 28 years. And for a time things went smoothly on the surface. When the St. Regis Hotel opened in 1905 the Lehrs gave a dinner so large that the table stretched from end to end of two dining rooms, and the couple had phones installed at either end so they could talk to one another.

But Harry's star was on the decline. The beginning of the decline may have dated from one day shortly after 1900 when, attending the New York Horse Show, he approached the box in which Alice Roosevelt Longworth, an acquaintance and the daughter of the President of the United States, was sitting. Harry saluted her. Mrs. Longworth stared straight in front of her, giving no sign of recognition. Then she turned away and adjusted her hat. Redfaced, Harry hurried away. He had been snubbed. In public. That was not an insignificant occurrence in those days.

In 1910 he had a nervous breakdown. He returned to Baltimore to recover. Two years later the Lehrs moved to Paris, where they remained during the First World War, with Harry doing his part by giving teas for the American soldiers. In 1919 he announced that he was retiring from Society altogether.

He was still in the habit of having lunch every day at the Ritz, where he always sat at the same window table, the better to see and be seen. But Mrs. Lehr eventually tired of allowing him even this sop to his vanity. One day a member of the family went to see M. Ollivier, the famous maitre d'hotel of the Ritz, to say that Harry should not be extended any more credit, as he was no longer in a position to afford such extravagances as luncheon at the Ritz (the $25,000 allowance must have dried up).

M. Ollivier rose to the occasion with true French gallantry. "Mr. Lehr," he said, "will continue to be, as he has always been, welcome at the Ritz, where I shall be honored in the future if he will consider himself as my guest. Please inform Mr. Lehr that his favorite table by the window will be reserved for him tomorrow as usual."

In 1927 Harry, ill, returned to Baltimore for a brain operation at Johns Hopkins Hospital. At the end of 1928 he returned once more from Paris, this time to die. His wife did not accompany him. He died on January 3, 1929, that year when so many things came to an end. Two days later his funeral was held at St. Ignatius Church, just around the corner from Mount Vernon Place. There were no pallbearers.

Poor Harry.

Poor Mount Vernon Place.

They had gone down together, so to speak. In the case of Mount Vernon Place the causes were many. Even as Walter Poultney was making his statement about giving the people pleasure, in 1913, some of the seeds were sown. Because of one amendment to the Constitution, just passed, income tax was coming in, inevitably to reduce the money-making power of the rich. Because of another amendment, also just passed, United States Senators were for the first time being elected by the people instead of the state legislatures, making the government a step more democratic. The lamps were about to go out in Europe, and when they came on after the Great War they never burned quite so brightly in the palaces again. But if, on that bright Sunday in 1913, the upper classes had any idea that their world was about to fade and Mount Vernon Place with it, they gave no sign.

For a time, indeed, all seemed well, or almost well. In 1916 Mayor James H. Preston called for improvements to the four parks, and the following year Thomas Hastings came to Baltimore from the New York firm of Carrere and Hastings to re-landscape. He was one of the finest landscape architects in the country.

The semicircular walkways in the parks were straightened; the fountain in South Washington Place, known as the lily fountain, was replaced by the present one and that park was completely redesigned; trees and shrubbery were planted, and the sculptures were placed in their present positions.

Hastings did a good job, but as usual changes encountered their opponents. The Women's Civic League objected when the statue of Severn Teackle Wallis lay on the ground, crated, for some time, its fate undecided. Architect Francis Jencks, whose parents lived at One West, recalls that his father was "apoplectic" over the re-landscaping, partly because it seemed inappropriate to spend money in such a fashion in the midst of a war. But the objections raised over the re-landscaping were as nothing compared to the furies loosed by two other changes: the placing of benches in the parks for the first time, and the location of the new Lafayette statue just south of the Washington Monument.

The first benches appeared on August 15, 1915. It was not long before the outcry reached the newspapers. One citizen wrote that it was uncomfortable to walk in the squares now, when *anyone at all* could sit on the benches and gaze at one. Miss Marie Louise Welsh, who lived on Washington Place, complained that, "the place has become an open-air sleeping porch, picnic ground and courting center for careless or ill-mannered people," and *The Sun* reported that "her words but express the sentiment of many concerning what they regard as the desecration of a shrine of beauty."

The paper's editorial position on this burning issue was ambiguous, however. An editorial on the matter first took the residents to task with a couple of not-too-gently ironical sentences which sound as if they were written by Mencken: "Since the White House has been invaded by common men like Lincoln, Garfield and others without a coat of arms to their backs, and since many other rude representatives of the 'lower social strata' have contracted the pernicious habit of forcing their way to the front in public life, finance, industry, medicine, law and religion, without regard to the rules of the Herald's College, it is difficult to enforce the old regulations which made for decent decorum and precedence. No matter where you go now, you are brought into contact, more or less intimate, with the 'lower orders' and there is even a dreadful possibility that those not in our set may crowd against us in the other world."

But at its end the editorial seemed to support removal of the benches; Mount Vernon Place, it said, "should be protected from anything that would mar [its]. . . , character, not merely because of the private protests of residents, but because of public self-respect and because of reverence for what it represents. It is our municipal Pantheon, where we have enshrined the ideas that stand in the place of public gods, and for that reason it deserves to be held in special honor."

The Park Board, which had authorized the benches in the first place, voted unanimously that they should stay. And John D. Spencer, first branch City Councilman, fumed at the notion that people should not be allowed to sit there. "The aristocrats in this city are entirely too particular," he said. "The parks are for the poor people anyhow. The rich don't use 'em, and why shouldn't the boys and girls who have no other place to go use a park bench for the scene of their courting?"

The objections to them didn't die easily. In 1923 it was reported that many workmen went over there to eat their lunches, and in 1924 a resident complained of serenaders outside his window at 2 A.M.

On the other hand, the benches don't seem to have driven the residents out of the parks. A lady who lived on or near the squares for 50 years noted in 1970 that she and her friends used the benches in the Twenties. "The squares were meeting places," she said. "You sat or strolled there in the afternoon, met your friends and chatted with them."

Almost as great a controversy was aroused when the pedestal to hold the Lafayette statue (memorializing in his name the soldiers who had fallen in France in the First World War) was placed just south of the monument. No one, of course, objected to remembering the fallen heroes. When the returning Maryland soldiers arrived here in 1919 they marched triumphantly through the squares to the music of bands and the cheers of the crowds. In European fashion, the Jenckses at One West threw open their windows and hung their Oriental rugs on the balconies in colorful tribute. It was perhaps the first time Mount Vernon Place had seen such a contingent since 1845, when soldiers about to leave for the Mexican War had camped around the monument.

Aesthetics raised the opposition to Lafayette. Such a large pedestal, with such a large equestrian statue on it, would block the view of the base of the monument from the south, people said. Committees formed and Henry Walters, whose recently-completed gallery faced the south square, joined the fight against the statue. So did H. L. Mencken, who said it would look like "Washington's spitoon."

But Mr. Hastings, who had planned the location of the memorial, insisted that it was correct. Against all opposition — and local opposition had seldom failed against outside pressure for change — Mr. Hastings won, with happy results. The statue, seen from the south against the backdrop of the monument, enhances the view up Washington Place, which is probably the most-often-rendered view in Baltimore. At the memorial's dedication in 1924 President Coolidge spoke.

While all these changes were going on in full view, others took place behind the curtained facades. Blanchard Randall, who bought the Tiffany-Fisher house (8 West) in 1919, was one of the last prominent people to move in. More were moving out. One by one houses were converted to apartments, some with absentee landlords. Some of the buildings housed doctors' offices or business offices, tending to tilt the place away from the purely residential.

In 1929 Dr. A. D. McConachie, in a speech to a local improvement society, went so far as to call Mount Vernon Place degenerate. "It is a runway for dogs," he said. "At night it is a gathering place for nighthawks and wrens. There are no flowers and only sometimes is there grass. There are houses on Mount Vernon Place which no man here could be proud to know of. We have appealed to real estate men to remove these people, but at this time they are still there. These are the facts that the square is degenerate."

There was more than one reason for the decline. The servant problem must have been one. It was getting harder to get them and some people who lived on the squares could no longer afford enough servants to keep their houses properly.

Another cause may have been the growing commercialism of Charles Street. The blocks just south of Mount Vernon Place had changed almost entirely from residential to commercial, and the same was increasingly true to the north as well, at least along Charles Street.

Then there was the movement to the suburbs. Roland Park and Guilford were developed in the early part of this century, and just as the automobile made it easier to live in a suburb and get to work downtown every day, so the automobile, with its noise and fumes, made it less pleasant to live as near downtown as Mount Vernon Place.

There were people who predicted, with complacence or alarm, great changes for the four squares in the years to come. One of them was the great journalist Gerald W. Johnson. Writing in *The Sun* in 1929, he said: "Take Mount Vernon Place itself and consider how many of the houses facing upon it have been there as long as fifty years. Three or four, perhaps, were erected prior to 1878, but by far the larger number date from the nineties, or later. And of those now standing, how many will be in existence fifty years hence? It is highly probable that not one will be left. Even the Peabody Institute may acquire a new building before the year 1978."

It will do the late Mr. Johnson's illustrious reputation no harm to say that he was not only misinformed — most of the houses on Mount Vernon Place in 1929 had been there since before 1878 — but his prognostication was absolutely wrong. Not one building on any of the squares has been replaced since 1929. The most recent building is Peabody's Leakin Hall, completed in 1926. In a city, and an age, in which so much has changed in the last 50 years, and in a nation which traditionally has had little regard for its urban past, such a record is truly remarkable, indeed almost miraculous.

Why has it happened? It has happened because, whenever the squares were threatened, there were people, whether residents or not, who cared enough about them and what they represent to put up a fight, individually and by forming organizations.

The first preservation organization was the Municipal Art Society, formed by Theodore Marburg and others, which in 1904, it will be remembered, had succeeded in getting the state legislature to pass the zoning law limiting the height of buildings to 70 feet above the base of the monument.

There were many other fights, large and small, important and silly, in the years that followed. The forces supporting preservation of the status quo lost those over the benches and the Lafayette statue; others they won.

On October 14, 1922, a sign advertising a movie went up in West Mount Vernon Place. As soon as he heard about it Police Commissioner Charles Gaither dispatched a contingent of Baltimore's finest to take it down.

In 1923 there was an attempt to open a restaurant at 702 Cathedral Street, fronting on Mount Vernon Place. Dr. Henry Barton Jacobs, who lived in the largest mansion, expressed the feelings of his neighbors when he wrote: "It must be the aim of the state, the city and every inhabitant to guard and preserve these squares. The city has ample room for the extension of its business districts. Shall it not be the care of all to see that

The only chateauesque house on the squares is a record of a brief period in American architecture, in the 1890's, when wealthy men wanted their houses to look like those of French noblemen. Charles E. Cassell, the architect here, had a hard time squeezing this chateau onto a townhouse lot and making it look impressive at the same time, but he did his best. It has some wonderful rooms inside, especially the corner tower rooms.

78

This view of the west side of the north square shows prominently the Washington Apartments, by E.H. Glidden, erected 1906. The Beaux Arts building's owner sued in the courts over the 70-foot height limitation (enacted after the Stafford, next door, was built), but lost. So he made his building 69 feet, 8 inches tall. The ridiculous pipe on top detracts from the view of the building, and one would think that the residents, who are the owners, would do something about it.

"Sir" Walter Poultney, dressed for a costume ball; need one say more?

Harry Lehr, somewhere. It is not known who is with him. The lines in the picture are newspaper artist's crop marks which were not removed before it was re-photographed.

The boy with the turtle, by Crenier, gambols happily in the west square fountain. He was a 1916 addition to the 1880's fountain.

The naiad in the east square fountain, by well-known Baltimore artist Grace H. Turnbull, was presented to the city by the Women's Civic League and placed in 1962.

There was a great hue and cry when this statue of Lafayette, a memorial to the soldiers of World War I, was placed in front of the Washington Monument in the early 1920's. The work, by Andrew O'Connor (1924), has great drama as it prances into the air over the south square, and Lafayette, seen from below, looks down his nose at you with a perfect expression of haughty nobility.

In the south square fountain is the sea urchin. The original of this bronze was by Edward Berge, but it was too small in scale for the fountain. In 1961 Henry Berge completed this large version, donated to the city by Frederick R. Huber. The smaller one now graces a pool at Hopkins University's Homewood campus, where it looks entirely at home.

The statue of Severn Teackle Wallis, for whom Wallis Warfield was named, was executed by Laurent Marqueste in 1903. After the re-landscaping of 1916-1918, it was placed in its present position in the east square, looking east across Monument Street.

The Flower Mart was initiated in 1911, and held around the Washington Monument once a year through 1970. In that year, however, a melee caused by teenagers led to arrests and the next year the mart was moved downtown. Fortunately it has since returned to Mount Vernon Place, where it is held one day in early May each year. This picture is from the Teens, and is interesting for the long-dressed women, the policeman with his round-topped hat near the gate on the near left, the rattan chair hanging from the cover of a booth in the left background, and the boy in knickers with a package under his arm in the right background. One can also see that they used a lot of palm fronds as decoration. The round-globed street lights are a change from those on the east square in the first picture in this book (ca. 1900).

This is the proposed Walters Art Gallery, an architect's sketch published before the loans of 1958 and 1960 for its construction were defeated by Douglas Gordon and others. It shows that almost the entire block of the south side of West Mount Vernon Place, from One West to the corner of Cathedral Street, would have been demolished for the addition to the Walters. Included in the demolition would have been the Walters house at 5 West and the Garrett-Jacobs mansion, now the Engineering Center of Baltimore, at 7, 9, and 11 West.

The houses across from East Mount Vernon Place, on the southeast corner of St. Paul and Monument Streets. These houses, which provided a properly-scaled enclosing presence for the east square, were torn down in the 1960's for a proposed development which never took place. As a result, they are gone and there has been an empty space there for almost 15 years.

This glorious picture of the St. James Hotel at the southwest corner of Centre and Charles Streets shows it in full Victorian flower. Though at the end of its life it was painted white, it was a nice building to have across from South Washington Place for two reasons: it was an example of a particular Nineteenth Century style not seen on the four squares themselves, and it was not out of scale. The lumpish apartment house which replaced it in the 1960's is in no way appropriate.

these quiet spots shall be passed by and allowed to remain the peaceful abiding place of the great Washington?..." The restaurant did not open.

The fight to prevent the building of the tall Mount Vernon Place Apartments at the corner of Cathedral and Monument Streets was lost in 1929, but in 1932, when Mrs. James H. Dorsey donated a sapling elm to be placed in the north square, she caused the biggest fuss over a tree that Baltimore has ever seen. The year was Washington's bicentennial, and the sapling was an offshoot of the elm under which Washington was supposed to have taken command of the Continental Army in Cambridge, Massachusetts, 157 years before. It was planted right in the center of the north square, but it wasn't there a week before someone said that when it grew up it would obstruct the view of the monument from the north.

Mrs. Dorsey replied that it wouldn't obstruct the view of the *top* of the monument, and that, besides, she had grown many such saplings from offshoots of the same tree, had donated them to states across the country, and nobody had ever failed to appreciate her saplings before. But public sentiment was too strong. The parks department removed the tree and replanted it in a spot near Druid Hill Park's Washington monument.

Earlier the same year banker and newspaper publisher Harry Black anonymously donated $15,000 for planting in the squares, and this was accepted with thanks. Japanese cherry trees were chosen, and for a few years the squares were all abloom in the spring. But the trees were replaced in 1945, whether because they were dying or because of opposition to things Japanese is not known.

In 1939 Dr. Jacobs died, his wife having predeceased him by three years. They had no heirs, and so the great mansion at 7, 9 and 11 West was sold at auction. It went, for a fraction of its assessment, to a funeral establishment. The funeral establishment hardly got the check written before public pressure forced a sale to the Boumi Temple, which owned it for the next 20 years until the Engineering Society bought it.

In the early Forties there was a serious urban renewal plan to tear down all the houses and erect in their place multi-story apartment buildings. Theodore Marburg made a plea for the status quo:

"Mount Vernon Place is not a very wide park," he said. "High buildings would seriously interfere with its charm. It is not only a question of the height of the buildings marring the appearance of the square. What is needed in cities is sunlight.... The expense of gardens in the city, because of taxes, makes it necessary to build in solid rows. Due to this, it is even more necessary to realize that we cannot have too many breathing spaces with grass and shrubbery, to supply the country element....

"We must, perhaps, look forward to business houses appearing on Mount Vernon Place in time, but the skyline....should not be further sacrificed."

By this time, however, Mount Vernon and Washington Places had their greatest champion of modern times in the person of Douglas H. Gordon, Jr. Mr. Gordon, though he has never lived on Mount Vernon Place, is the descendant of those Gordons who built several of its houses. As such, he had a proprietary interest in the area, and in the 1930's, seeing the way things were going, he formed a plan based on his own theory, which he calls the Gordon Curve.

"Living on Chase Street," he said later, "I walked downtown every day, and. . . . I was noticing that buildings were being torn down 70 years after they were built. For example, the Governor's Mansion in Annapolis was built in 1866 and virtually torn down in 1936, just 70 years later. The Court of Appeals building more recently was ordered torn down in 1972, just 70 years after it was built. The Jacobs house, which the barbarians wanted to tear down in 1958 and again in 1960 [for an extension of the Walters Art Gallery] was built just 70 years before.

"Noticing such things, I developed the Gordon Curve, which states that when a building is new we rate it at 100 per cent. It then deteriorates in public esteem at a rate of 1½ per cent a year, until, at 70 years old, when it's just grandma's style, and the plumbing and heating are wearing out, everybody's down on it. That's when it's most likely to be torn down. On the other hand, if it survives that low point on the Gordon Curve it starts rising rather rapidly and in 30 years it's back to par when it's 100 years old. Witness the City Hall, which was just 100 years old when it was restored in the 1970's.

"Well, I already had this curve in mind when I founded the Mount Vernon Improvement Association in 1938. . . . I decided that if I could hold the fort for 25 years, natural forces — the Gordon Curve — would preserve. . . [the buildings] more or less automatically after that."

The Mount Vernon Improvement Association was for the preservation of the whole area, not just the four squares; but preserving the area meant preserving the squares as the keystone. Over the next 35 years Mr. Gordon, a lawyer, went to court some 300 times, by his own account, in zoning battles. Most of the time he won.

His biggest fight was over the Garrett-Jacobs mansion, which the city proposed to tear down, along with the two houses west of it to the corner of Cathedral Street, in order to build a wing on the gallery. Joining forces with Dr. Hugh Francis Hicks (who now owns four properties on the four squares) and others, Mr. Gordon launched a campaign to defeat a $9,000,000 loan on the ballot in 1958, which would have provided the money for the Walters wing.

Fighting almost the whole Establishment of Baltimore, including the *Sunpapers,* Mr. Gordon obtained the right to open the house to the public before election day, so as to let people see what they were going to lose. Due to that and other tactics, the loan was defeated by two to one, one of the first municipal loans ever defeated in Baltimore.

In 1960 the city came back with another proposal, this time scaled down to $4,000,000, and again Douglas Gordon and his forces succeeded in defeating it. After that there were no more attempts to put the Walters wing on Mount Vernon Place, and when there was an eventual proposal for $1,000,000, to help the Walters build the wing at the corner of Centre and Cathedral Streets, off of Mount Vernon Place, Mr. Gordon did not oppose it and it passed.

Using what he terms "Scientific Obstructionism," Mr. Gordon managed to preserve Mount Vernon Place and much of the surrounding area until the Gordon Curve on it could rise again. He had his enemies, and has often been called abrasive; but he, a conservative, was an urban preservationist long before urban preservation became the darling of liberals in the 1960's; and all Baltimore owes him a debt of gratitude for what he did to keep Mount Vernon Place untouched and the adjacent area as largely residential as possible.

In 1964, Mr. Gordon's aims became city policy for the first time, when the newly formed Commission for Historical and Architectural Preservation was given jurisdiction over the exteriors of buildings on all four squares. After that no owner could change a facade without the approval of the commission.

One of the commission's first big battles was over the four houses at the end of the south side of East Mount Vernon Place, numbers 27-33 East. The houses (all of which, as you will remember, once belonged to the Caton sisters) were bought by the Peabody Institute in 1962. A few years later the Institute proposed tearing them down for a park to serve as the entrance to its new dormitory complex by Edward Durrell Stone, behind. CHAP refused to allow the destruction, saying that a park facing a park would not be as appropriate to the design of Mount Vernon Place as the houses. When the Institute came back with a proposal to tear the houses down and erect a wall in their place, CHAP again refused permission, and the refusal stuck. A victory for the preservation of Mount Vernon Place, it was also CHAP's first major victory. Since then CHAP's jurisdiction has grown to include a number of other areas of the city. Since then, the Peabody has made no more attempts to tear the houses down, and now says that it has plans for their eventual renewal as offices and other spaces for the use of the Institute. At any rate, Peabody assures, the facades will be preserved.

Things were looking up for Mount Vernon Place until the riots of 1968 left people with doubts about moving into the city. Two years later the annual Flower Mart, held around the base of the monument early in May and a tradition since 1911, was disrupted by a melee in which 50 youths were arrested and at least 16 others were hospitalized. The following year the Flower Mart moved downtown to Charles Center, and there were more doubts about Mount Vernon Place.

Some people left. But others, such as Mr. Gladding at One West and the Leroy Hoffbergers at 16 East, stayed. Dr. Hicks was offered two of the four properties he owns, at 12 and 20 East, for $60,000 to $70,000, and bought them. The Engineering Society held on to the Garrett-Jacobs mansion and continued its admirable restoration of the property, which has so far cost the society $1,500,000. The Mount Vernon Club stuck with the beautiful Tiffany-Fisher house, which it has preserved so well; the location of this very exclusive club on Mount Vernon Place brings to the square many socially prominent people, some of whose forebears lived there. Dr. Iliff, now retired, still owns 14 West, where his son and others practice ophthalmology.

In recent years number 3 West, formerly Eastern College, has been turned into attractive condominium apartments. The handsome Washington Apartments have remained popular, and recently have drawn a number of new residents who have lavishly redecorated some of the units. The future of the building looks good. Number 718 Washington Place, the chateau at the corner of Madison Street, has been bought by one or more people from Washington and redone at considerable expense. There is a rumor that the house has been offered to the city as a residence for the mayor, in return for a tax writeoff; but the rumor was not confirmed as of the summer of 1983.

There are problem spots. Some of the neighbors regret that the Stafford Hotel has become low-income housing. Some of the brownstones on East Mount Vernon Place are still cut up into little apartments, and appear to be in sad shape. And there are still the loungers on those benches, which continue to draw their share of derelicts to sleep in almost any weather. Recently the city drastically lowered the height of the bushes on South Washington Place because of residents' fears that they were lurking places for criminals.

If Douglas Gordon was successful in most of his battles, he could not prevent the demolition almost 15 years ago of the houses on the southeast corner of Monument and St. Paul Streets, leaving a large gap as one looks down East Mount Vernon Place. Worse, no one could or would prevent the destruction of the delightful old St. James Hotel, just across from South Washington Place on the southwest corner of Centre and Charles Streets. In its place was erected a lumpish apartment building whose wall-like facade facing Washington Place virtually destroys the view for anyone looking south from the base of the monument.

But it must be remembered that Mount Vernon Place, like any urban area, has always had its problems, and unlike most it has survived them. Back in the Nineteenth Century geese at one time became such a problem that they were prohibited on the squares. As long ago as the 1840's, when frequent riots in the streets earned Baltimore the nickname "Mobtown," the mobs often chose the site of the monument for their gatherings. As Herbert M. Brune, then living at 16 East, wrote in 1943:

"With political parties and groups such as the Know-Nothings trying to control elections by force, rival gangs roamed the city and overran the better neighborhoods. Street fights broke out on Mount Vernon Place and at the foot of the monument. . . . It is perhaps worthwhile to recall that the great era of social supremacy of Mount Vernon Place began shortly after this time of terrorism and degradation. Today. . . .old residents need not fear that there is no hope of recovery. For the conditions with which their ancestors had to cope were far worse than any problem which faces them today or which is likely to face them in the future." Mr. Brune could write those words today with equal justification.

On the whole, people who know Mount Vernon Place seem to think things are looking up. The Flower Mart came back in 1981. Dr. Hicks sees the day when most of the houses will be turned into condominium apartments as 3 West has been, and when the number of apartments allowed in each house will be smaller. In 1977 Mr. Gordon, thinking of the whole Mount Vernon area, said, "Five years ago I felt that my 34 years' work was almost in vain; but I don't think so now....A group of young people are coming into the area who can't afford these terribly expensive suburban houses but who can afford to buy an old house downtown, partly restore it, occupy perhaps half of it and rent out the rest. I think sooner or later the eyesores in the way of parking lots on Charles Street will be covered with apartments, and then Charles Street will not look like a bombed city. It will look in some ways like the city I was born in."

In 1959 John Osman, then vice president of the Ford Foundation's fund for adult education, spoke here and summed up what Mount Vernon Place means to those who are familiar with it. "You have a civilization here," he said simply. Forty years before another visitor had said much the same thing.

If you had happened to be strolling on Mount Vernon Place on a certain day early in the year 1921, you would likely have noticed a large, fat man with a walrus mustache and a pair of glasses that almost disappeared into his huge face. He was G. K. Chesterton, the English writer, and being a writer he was sensitive to the almost palpable presence of history that is as much a part of Mount Vernon Place as the buildings or the statues. Like Henry James before him, Chesterton fell in love with Baltimore, and was prompted to write this about his visit:

"I hear some New Yorkers refer to Philadelphia and Baltimore as 'dead towns.' They mean by a dead town a town that has had the impudence not to die. And what I mean by Philadelphia and Baltimore being alive is precisely what those people mean by their being dead; it is continuity; it is the presence of the life first breathed into them and of the purpose of their being; it is the benediction of the founders of the colonies and the fathers of the Republic....

"On the top of a hill on one side of the town stood the first monument raised after the revolution to Washington. Beyond it was [the base of] a new monument saluting in the name of Lafayette the American soldiers who fell fighting in France in the Great War. Between them were steps of stone seats, and I sat down on one of them....

"Sitting there on that stone step under the quiet sky I had some experience of the thronging of thousands of living thoughts and things, noisy and numberless as birds, that give its everlasting vivacity and vitality to a dead town."

I believe it is that sense more than any other which has led people to preserve the physical presence of Mount Vernon Place, so that the metaphysical presence will remain as well. If that is true, then we can believe in its future.

The last word should go to one of its distinguished residents, Dr. Henry Barton Jacobs, who some 60 years ago wrote: "The present residents of these squares will pass away, their interest will cease, but the squares, if preserved, and the monument will live on through countless generations, still the pride of all Baltimoreans."

1

In the 1920's etchings were as much in vogue as posters are today. Mount Vernon Place, then as always, was the most popular Baltimore subject. Here we see six views, from various points, by: Gabriélle deVeaux Clements (1), Anton Schutz (2), Karoly & Szanto (3), M. Paul Roche (4), Edwin Tunis (5), and John McGrath (6). The stronger of these are the Clements (one of a now highly-desired set of eight Baltimore views she executed in the Twenties), the Schutz for its detail, and the Tunis for its unusual high viewpoint. The weakest is obviously the flat, dead view by Karoly and Szanto, a virtual copy of another view by Clements. Its redeeming value is its detail. It seems appropriate to end our essay with these efforts by some of the many artists whose work has depicted Mount Vernon Place over the years.

2

3

4

5

6

c. 1900 Henry Walters buys all 4 houses, 1905 demolishes for Walters Art Gallery by Delano and Aldrich.	**600** 1845, Richard Norris; George Somerville Norris, Mr. and Mrs. Orville Horwitz.	1843, James Howard McHenry to Greenway; Greenway to Robert Campbell; 1860, Zenus Barnum; 1872, Annie Barnum Gordon to Andrew Reid; 1899, Reid to Alexander Shaw; 1901 to John K. Shaw; 1905, to Oscar Turner; 1909, to Evalyn S. France; 1927, Joseph I. and Tatiana France to Georgia Gelston Jones; 1929, Women's City Club of Baltimore; 1942, John and Lucille Matthews; 197?, to Joseph Azola; 1976, Azola to Vernon and Shirley Wiesand. **15**
	602 1853, Miss Eliza Toy's boarding house; Michael Jenkins.	Mr. and Mrs. Perry, James Hooper, Mr. and Mrs. Henry Pratt Janes (by 1884); 1913, Mrs. Henry Barton Jacobs; 1940, Boumi Temple (owner); 1962, Engineering Society of Baltimore (owner); Estelle Dennis Dance Studio (present occupant). **13**
	604 Stephen S. Lee; Sarah F. Lee; McCoy family; Mrs. Turnbull's boarding house.	**11** Samuel K. George; 1872, to Mr. and Mrs. Robert Garrett as wedding present from John W. Garrett. / **9** Captain and Mrs. James Ryan (Mrs. Ryan nee Susan Fitzhugh Gordon). / **7** Mr. and Mrs. Basil Gordon? (according to various accounts; Douglas Gordon says no); William W. Taylor. — 1884, Mr. and Mrs. Garrett, owners of 11 West, buy 9 West, hire Stanford White to combine two houses into one; 1902, Mrs. Henry Barton Jacobs (formerly widow of Robert Garrett) buys 7 West, hires John Russell Pope to add it to her mansion; 1940, after deaths of Jacobses, sold briefly to William Cook Funeral Home, then to Boumi Temple; 1962, to Engineering Society of Baltimore.
	606 1846, son of architect Benjamin Latrobe; (possibly designed by Niernsee); Mrs. Turnbull's boarding house (with 604); residents are said to have included younger Jerome Bonaparte and Woodrow Wilson.	1847, John H. Duval; 1871, to William Walters; 1894, to Henry Walters at death of William; 1931, to city at death of Henry; now offices of Walters Art Gallery.
		1850's, John Nelson, attorney General of Maryland; boarding house?; Joseph Williams; Mr. and Mrs. Thomas Poultney; William F. Burns; Mr. and Mrs. Joseph McEvoy; Red Cross (World War II); Eastern College of Commerce (Edgar Berman, owner); condominium apartments (present).
		Nicholas Hitzelberger had small house on site, perhaps 1820; his daughter Mary lived with him and his granddaughter, Virginia, born there 1833; 1849 Mr. and Mrs. John Hanson Thomas (Mrs. Thomas nee Annie Campbell Gordon) build present house to design by Niernsee and Neilson; 1892, to Mr. and Mrs. Francis Jencks, alterations by architect Charles Platt; 1953, Mrs. Jencks dies, house bought by city; 1962, city sells to Harry Lee Gladding; 1982, Gladding offers house for sale.

WASHINGTON PLACE SOUTH

Peabody Institute now owns all five houses.	**601** Thomas H. Morris (Nineteenth Century). / **603** McKim Marriott; Dr. Charles Shippen; James Carroll; the Misses Milligan; Mrs. Robert Bancroft. / **605** Drs. B. F. Coy and McPherson, dentists (20th Century). / **607** Joseph H. Snyder; John M. Highe. / **609** 1854, built by Duer family; Mrs. John Duer; Mr. and Mrs. Wade; James H. Merrill; John S. Wright; Mr. Warfield; Richard Gittings; 1912, Samuel S. Keyser; 1913, Mrs. Walter W. Abell; 1950, John D. Schapiro.	Bevan and Sons marble yard (1815?). John Pendleton Kennedy (author, etc.), 1830's and after. Josias Pennington (architect), before Peabody. — 1859, ground broken for Peabody Institute building; first three bays completed (architect, Edmund G. Lind) before 1862, but institute does not open until 1868; final four bays of original building, containing library, completed 1878. **1-2**
		Granville Oldfield; Miss Gwynn; the Misses Bond girls' school; Miss Carman's boarding house; Peabody acquired 1915 for preparatory school. — Leakin Hall (Peabody Preparatory building) completed 1926.
		1850's and before, 29-33 owned by Caton sisters, granddaughters of Charles Carroll of Carrollton; three of sisters, known as "Three Graces", married English nobility; fourth sister, Emily McTavish, remained in Baltimore and may have resided in one of the houses. 1962, Peabody acquires all four houses (27-33). — Residents unknown; may have been house of prostitution, 1930's or 1940's. **2**
		Capt. William Owens, 1850's; Ellen Atkinson; Mr. and Mrs. George Whitelock. **2**
		George William Brown (mayor of Baltimore, 1861); George Mister; W. Hall Harris, Sr. and W. Hall Harris, Jr., until 1940's. **3**
		Robert McLane (later governor of Maryland), 1850's; 1860's, A. S. Abell; Charles J. M. Gwinn; James H. Preston, mayor of Baltimore. **3**

Who Lived Where
A Partial List of Residents — Not Necessarily Owners

18 Chancellor Johnson; William Murdoch (or Murdock); Henry White; 1895, Severn Apartments, designed by Charles E. Cassell (entrance on Cathedral street).

16 1887, Edward Didier (house designed by Charles L. Carson, loggia addition by Joseph Evans Sperry, 1896); Alexander Winchester; Mr. and Mrs. Thomas Poultney; Alexander Brown; David Bartlett (1920's); Dr. H. F. Hicks, present owner (apartments).

14 Designed by Josias Pennington; Mr. and Mrs. George Small; Mr. and Mrs. George Tiffany; William Tiffany; 1897, Theodore Marburg; Charles and Grainger Marburg; Dr. Charles E. Iliff, present owner (doctors' offices).

12 Mr. and Mrs. Alexander Gordon (built before 1847); Mr. and Mrs. J. Hall Pleasants; Dr. and Mrs. Edgar Berman (1950's-1960's); Mr. and Mrs. Harvey Kayne. House possibly altered 1860 and/or 1871 by Edmund G. Lind.

8 1842, William Tiffany; 1851, Elise and George Tiffany; 1863, Allston Club; 1865, Miss S. A. Kummer's School for Young Ladies; 1877, Dr. and Mrs. Henry Hupfeld; 1889, Dr. and Mrs. Thomas Deford; 1898, Judge and Mrs. William A. Fisher; 1901, Judge Fisher dies—1901-1919, house occupied at various times by Mrs. Fisher, her mother Mrs. Este, her son William A. Fisher, Jr., her daughter and son-in-law Senator and Mrs. William Cabell Bruce; 1919, Mr. and Mrs. Blanchard Randall; 1941, Mount Vernon Town Club (present Mount Vernon Club); original architect unknown, late 1890's interior alterations by Henry Randall for Judge and Mrs. Fisher, further alterations to interior for Blanchard Randalls.

6 Lambert Gittings; O. F. Bresee; Mr. and Mrs. William F. Cochran (c.1904); Italian Consulate; English Speaking Union (present).

Greenway House: see Washington Apartments, 700 Washington Place.

718 George Graham, built in 1893; Isabella Graham-Hughes, until the 1970's; John King (present).

710 Dr. William A. Moale; Dr. Moale tore down his house to build Stafford Hotel, opened Nov. 5, 1894. Now Stafford apartments.

700 1835, Edward McDonald Greenway, Sr. (house faced Mount Vernon Place); Edward McDonald Greenway, Jr.; 1906, Washington Apartments, designed by E. H. Glidden for William Cochran. Bought by General Robert Gill, 1950; now co-operative apartments.

WASHINGTON PLACE NORTH

1829, Charles Howard; James Wilson; Mr. and Mrs. Gambrill; 1870, Mount Vernon Place Methodist Church, designed by Dixon and Carson.

10 Albert Schumacher; George A. Von Lingen; Mr. and Mrs. Charles E. Reiman (1901-1956); Asbury House of Mount Vernon Place Methodist Church (present); house designed by Niernsee and Neilson, interior altered 1890's.

12 Colonel Richard E. France; Charles J. M. Eaton; Mrs. Edward White; composer Hugh Newsom resident, 20th Century; carriage house behind was studio of artist Trafford Klots, 1930's-1970's; Dr. H. F. Hicks present owner of house and carriage house (apartments).

14 Colonel Charles Carroll; 1863, Mr. and Mrs. Wilson Patterson (Betsy Patterson connection?); 1878, Miss McConky's boarding house; Mrs. Jeanne Galkin (present).

16 Mount Vernon Institute, run by Mrs. Andrew Jones, Sr.; Robert and/or John W. Garrett?; 1880's, Mrs. George Small; Mrs. Edwin F. Abell; advertising agency; 1943, Mr. and Mrs. Herbert M. Brune, Jr.; Leroy E. Hoffberger (present).

18 Otho Holland Williams; Mr. and Mrs. Leigh Bonsal; Lutheran Board of Foreign Ministers; Junior League of Baltimore; Mr. and Mrs. Richard O'Brien; Mr. and Mrs. Earle K. Shawe.

20 Samuel Revell; G. W. C. Whiting; Mrs. Frank E. Stickney.

22 Mrs. Victor Smith; Mrs. Edgeworth Bird.

24 William A. Moale, 1856; 1862, sold to Col. France; original house demolished for brownstone row; 1863, Colonel and Mrs. Walter Franklin.

26 Mrs. Daniel B. Dorsey (Nineteenth Century); John Y. James.

28 McCormick family; Mr. and Mrs. Walter B. Brooks (Nineteenth Century).

1862, Col. R. E. France buys 6 lots, builds row of brownstones, sells all 6, 1863.

719 Mr. Voss, father of Joseph Voss; Horatio L. Whitridge; his daughters, Mrs. Nisbet Turnbull and Mrs. T. Harrison Garrett; Mrs. Andrew Gregg and son Maurice (died 1942).

717 c. 1860, Penniman family; Thomas Lanahan (living there, 1908) added top story; William Lanahan; Eugene H. Beer; John Carroll Dunn; Dr. Hugh Francis Hicks, present owner (his offices and apartments; electric lighting museum in basement).

715 1850, Denmead family built house; Duers; 1880's or 1890's, Joshua Harvey, enlarged house and changed facade (originally all three houses looked like 719); Francis B. Harvey; 1950's, Dr. DeMarco; Dr. Charles Edwards (present).

Illustration Credits

About the Author

John Dorsey is a native of Baltimore, and a graduate of Gilman School and Harvard College. From 1962 to 1981 he was a member of the staff of the Sunday Sun *as a feature writer concentrating on the arts and subjects relating to Baltimore history. He was also for two years book review editor and for ten years restaurant critic for the* Sunday Sun. *He is the co-author (with James D. Dilts) of* A Guide to Baltimore Architecture, *now in its second edition; and the editor of* On Mencken, *a volume of essays and Mencken selections published by Alfred A. Knopf in 1980 on the occasion of the Mencken centennial.*

Mount Vernon Place *is the tenth book on Baltimore and Maryland architecture and history published by Maclay & Associates since 1981.* Cover and title page design: Stanley Mossman.